VOICES OF THE WISC

LETTERS
FROM THE
FRONT
1898 – 1945

★

MICHAEL E. STEVENS
Editor

SEAN P. ADAMS   ELLEN D. GOLDLUST
Assistant Editors

Center for Documentary History
STATE HISTORICAL SOCIETY OF WISCONSIN
Madison: 1992

LIBRARY OF CONGRESS CATALOGING-IN-PUBLICATION DATA
Letters from the Front, 1898–1945. (Voices of the Wisconsin Past.)
Michael E. Stevens, editor. Sean P. Adams and Ellen D. Goldlust, assistant
editors.
Includes bibliographical references and index.
1. United States—History, Military—20th Century—Sources.
2. Soldiers—United States—Correspondence.
3. United States—Armed Forces—Military Life—History—20th Century—
Sources.
I. Stevens, Michael E. II. Adams, Sean P. III. Goldlust, Ellen D.
IV. State Historical Society of Wisconsin. V. Series

E745.L48 1992   92-27598 CIP   ISBN 0-87020-268-5

Contents

Introduction

"I'm not going to tell my mother what I have seen and gone through here in France"
— Paul Lappley, April 10, 1919

Sergeant Paul Lappley of Middleton, Wisconsin, had experienced enough war for a lifetime. Like many other veterans who had seen the carnage up close, he hoped to forget the horrors he had encountered in Europe. This volume is premised on an opposite belief — that war, with all its problems and contradictions, cannot and should not be forgotten. *Letters from the Front, 1898–1945* is a documentary history of the men and women from Wisconsin who participated in three foreign wars during an era in which the United States rose to the status of a dominant world power. This book differs from conventional military histories in that the story is told through the words of ordinary men and women who took part in these conflicts. The stories found here are not of battles or of grand strategies; politicians and generals do not figure in this account. Instead, the volume explores how wartime experiences changed the day-to-day lives of men and women from Wisconsin and how these people viewed those changes. The letters personalize the three wars and provide answers to questions not found in many traditional accounts. Were soldiers scared in combat? What did "no-man's-land" look like? What did it feel like to be on a bombing run? How did soldiers react to hearing news of the end of hostilities?

Voices of the Wisconsin Past is a series that presents first-person narratives of aspects of the state's history. Drawn from letters, diaries, oral histories, newspapers, and other accounts, the volumes supply a view of the past from the vantage point of the participants. The texts emphasize the ordinary citizens of the state and offer an account unmediated by the historian's narrative. They provide the reader with a sense of the authentic voices of the participants.

This particular volume began as part of efforts in Wisconsin to commemorate the fiftieth anniversary of the Second World War. It was quickly decided that the World War II experience could best be understood in a comparative light. Nearly 500,000 citizen-soldiers from Wisconsin participated in the Spanish-American War, World War I, and World War II, and during this time significant changes

v

occurred in both the state and the nation. Relatively few Wisconsin residents fought in the Spanish-American War. Only 5,500 Wisconsin men saw military service, and many of them were still in training camps when the war ended. Even fewer fought during the related Philippine Insurrection, which continued until 1902, although exact statistics are difficult to obtain. Precise casualty figures during the Spanish-American War also are hard to come by, but between 100 and 200 Wisconsin men died in the conflict.

World War I was a different case. With the state's large German-American population, there was strong sentiment against entry into the war, even among the state's political leadership. Nine of the state's eleven congressmen and one of the state's two senators voted against the declaration of war. Nonetheless, more than 120,000 Wisconsin residents served in the military, nearly 4,000 gave their lives, and more than 7,000 suffered wounds.

Of the three wars, the Second World War clearly had the greatest impact on the state and its citizens. Accordingly, more space in this volume has been devoted to the events of 1941–1945 than to the other two wars combined. About 350,000 Wisconsin men and women served in the armed forces. Of these, approximately 8,000 died and another 13,500 were wounded.

The sixty-two men and women whose letters are printed here are a diverse group. Although the writers include men like Billy Mitchell and Nathan Crook Twining, who pursued professional military careers, the great majority of the authors were citizen-soldiers who found themselves caught up in events larger than themselves. All the writers have a connection with Wisconsin, either being natives of the state or having lived in Wisconsin prior to their military service. In choosing letters for this volume, we have not attempted to print "typical" letters, which by their nature are routine, or to select letters that mirror a statistically accurate sample of the state's military population. Having reviewed thousands of letters from three wars, we instead chose those that most clearly articulate the diversity of experiences encountered by men and women in the service. This volume includes letters from enlisted men and officers, from draftees and volunteers, and from representatives of the various branches of service. The writers hailed from all over the state, from small communities such as Poplar in the northwest to metropolitan Milwaukee in the southeast. *Letters from the Front* contains more than simply letters from individuals in military or combat positions. We have selected letters written from U.S. training camps where young men and women prepared to go abroad and from individuals who aided soldiers at the front, including medics, nurses, Red Cross field workers, hospital recreation workers, and chaplains.

In this era of electronic mail, fax machines, and satellite transmission, it is easy to forget the importance of correspondence. Yet even in the recent Persian Gulf War, television news stories reminded us of the importance of letters to soldiers. They provided a link home for the GIs — a tie to stability and sanity while they were encountering a world gone awry. As many soldiers testified, mail was vital to morale.

To historians, wartime letters offer immediacy and a sense of the war from the perspective of citizen-soldiers who were uprooted from the office, the factory, or the farm to be called to duty. The letters are filled with fear and jaunty self-confidence; with boredom and excitement about new experiences; with an impatience with military ways and an understanding of the importance of the war. They range from a humorous 1918 tale of a young Milwaukee officer trying to order a meal in a small French café to a moving account written in 1943 by a pilot who survived a bombing raid that took the lives of more than half his squadron. There are letters from men who believed that they were fighting the war to end all wars as well as from a World War II vet who feared that his "kids are the ones who will have to sweat out the next little piece of hell." Not only do the letters provide a social history of adaptation to military life; they also offer insight into the emotional life of the men and women serving in the military.

The half-century between the Spanish-American War and the close of World War II saw substantial changes in American life, and these changes are reflected in the letters. Despite a growing trend toward imperialism, foreign affairs were considered inconsequential by most Americans in 1898, and few people would ever travel far from home. By 1945, men and women from Wisconsin had personal experience in places such as Normandy, Iwo Jima, Guadalcanal, and Dachau that five years earlier had been at most merely names in geography texts. The excitement about the glory of war found in letters from 1898 and 1917 was gone by 1918, when the slaughter of the Great War had become better known; by the 1940s it was almost entirely absent from the letters. The simple confidence of 1898 was replaced in 1945 by a less-naive view of a world that had produced a war that killed at least 40 million people.

The letters also reflect changing social beliefs. Attitudes of racial superiority conveyed in Spanish-American War letters contrast starkly with the joy expressed by a soldier during World War II about his participation in a racially integrated church service, although benighted attitudes about blacks and Asians remained common in the 1940s. The letters also reveal the leveling experience of military life. A young man from Middleton was surprised to find that his World War I unit contained two high school teachers, an engineer, and a millionaire who were washing dishes as well as a lawyer who was delivering mail. Each war saw an increased reliance on technology, and each innovation continued to amaze those in uniform. Whereas a new Krag-Jorgensen rifle that used smokeless powder dazzled Edward Niebuhr in Puerto Rico in 1898, Glenn Garlock was awestruck by the sight of forty airplanes in a single squadron in 1918. By 1943, U.S. Navy pilot A. Roger Conant found himself doing things daily that he once thought "were impossible to do in an airplane."

Although both attitudes and technology changed, much of military life remained the same. Men in uniform grew impatient with the "hurry up and wait" world of the military, whether in 1898, 1917, or 1941. Soldiers developed their own rituals that bonded groups of men into units in which each individual could rely on the other. Corporal Garlock's account of hazing new recruits in the Spanish-American War ("we are going to feed them on hard tack and sowbelly for a few days to break them in") has much in common with Lieutenant Louis Schauer's initiation as a "polliwog" when he first crossed the equator in 1943. Complaints about camp life were common, as evidenced by Garlock's grousing about monotony in 1898, Harry Trippe's griping about the food in 1917, or John Jenkins' "faint suspicion" in 1942 that movies "will be our only training in some phases of our military education."

Although the World War II generation was less likely to romanticize combat than its predecessors, veterans of all three wars quickly came to realize the horrors of war. War had lost its glamour for the men of La Crosse's Company M of the Third Regiment, who reported in 1898 that sickness had ravaged their unit and that they had only "fourteen men able to do light duty out of one hundred." A sense of the extent of the death and destruction is clear in nurse Margaret Rowland's 1918 description of "poor boys crying for their mothers and entreating you not to let them die so far from home" or Kenneth Worthing's 1945 letter describing Dachau as "almost too horrible to even try and imagine."

Once the fighting ended, veterans of all three wars demonstrated an understandable impatience to get on with their lives. Soldiers wanted home to be just as they remembered it as they returned to resume careers, education, and family life. Former prisoner-of-war Paul Fergot advised his wife not to "pay any attention to all the stories in magazines, etc, about the returning boys being strangers & having to be re-adapted. . . . They're just the same, and they want the folks at home to be just the same too." The war experience also left many men and women with a new sense of self-confidence. Peter Pappas wrote in 1943 from New Guinea, "I never dreamt I could do things that I now accept as commonplace."

The letters printed in this volume do not glorify war. As Captain Pappas wrote, "War is a matter of much training; constant repetition of fundamentals and a lot of hot, dirty work. There is no glamour to it." Wisconsin's war veterans hoped that their efforts were making a difference; certainly those who made the ultimate sacrifice would have hoped that their lives were not lost in vain. Along with this wish came the dream that the postwar world would be a better place. Writing from Germany in January, 1945, Roy Bergengren, Jr., put it best: "The lessons to be learned from war are so simple and so obvious, that they have to come out. This time, dammit, we've got to remember them."

*   *   *   *   *

In editing this volume, we have tried to preserve the sense of immediacy in letters often written under trying wartime conditions. Accordingly, they are reproduced exactly as written. We have not corrected grammar, spelling, capitalization, or punctuation, although we have standardized the date and place lines. Editorial insertions of words or letters always appear in brackets. Explanations of illegible text, such as *censored* or *torn,* appear in italic type and in brackets. Minor slips of the pen (e.g., repeated words as in "the the," transposed letters, or errors in typing) have been silently corrected. Minor changes in punctuation have been made only when absolutely necessary for clarity. These letters are often quite long and include references to family and local matters that are of no interest to the general reader. To include material from as many writers and on as many themes as possible, we have therefore excerpted many of the letters. Omissions are always noted with ellipsis marks. Citations to the original letters may be found in "Suggestions for Further Reading and Location of Original Letters" in the back of the volume. In most cases, the letters are from manuscripts held by the State Historical Society of Wisconsin.

*   *   *   *   *

The State Historical Society has been working to preserve the record of Wisconsin's history since 1846. Volumes in the *Voices of the Wisconsin Past* series would not have been possible without the donation of letters written during wartime. The Society continues to collect the letters of Wisconsin's veterans, from the territorial period through the Persian Gulf War. Persons wishing to discuss the donation of manuscript material are invited to contact the Archives Division at the State Historical Society of Wisconsin, 816 State Street, Madison, WI 53706.

Acknowledgments

This volume would not be possible without the generosity of the veterans whose letters appear here with their permission. We have made a concerted effort to locate the writers of the letters (or their families if they are deceased) and have been moved by their enthusiastic support for the project. This has come in the form of encouragement, donations of photographs and additional letters, background information, and financial contributions. We gratefully acknowledge the assistance of Duane F. Alexander, Stephen E. Ambrose, Roland Malcolm "Mac" Andresen, Sarah I. Barr, Margaret H. W. Bender, Rosemary Bergengren, Jon L. Boisclair, Janet Carlson, Elizabeth M. Casper, A. Roger Conant, Signe Skott Cooper, Donald B. Easum, Joyce Bong Erickson, Paul and Loa Fergot, Donna L. Fisker, Thurman Fox, Anne Hildt Geddes, Marcelle Gill, Donald Gocker, Dorothy Hartman, Paul E. Hassett, Daniel T. Hildt, David T. Hildt, J. Bradley Hildt, Le Roy Holm, Robert D. Isaksen, Josephine C. Jenkins, Elizabeth Schreiner Johnson, Evelyn Bernice Keenan, Margaret Ebert Kelk, Stuart Koch, John J. Koetting, Elizabeth G. Lee, Florence S. McCaffrey, John S. Marthaler, Cary Hildt Mathews, John R. Miller, John W. Moers, Lorraine Molner, Mildred Garlock Morris, Virginia Gates Munns, Eleanor A. Normington, Ole Oines, Peter G. Pappas, Carl Petrusha, Lyle G. Phillips, Jr., Merle N. Pickett, Eileen Pietrucha, John F. Polchinski, Jeannette Reddick, Mildred B. Rice, Louis Rodey, John S. Sammond, Luida E. Sanders, Louis A. Schauer, Joseph Schlicher, Carl Schluter, Eugene Simpson, Daniel Jordan Smith, Ellen G. Smith, Mark W. Smith, Marlyn Smith, Jane Thomas, Dorothy Radke Triggs, Eula Nee Twining, Merrill Twining, Robert B. Twining, Margaret Smith Walker, Vivian Croake Ward, Carl B. Weston, Charles E. White, John S. White, Nancy Smith Wilkey, Douglas Worthing, and Eunice S. Yeo.

We would also would like to thank the Portage County Historical Society for permitting use of a letter from Carl Jacobs in their collections, and Carroll College for permission to reprint the Charles King letters. Archivists Harry Miller of the State Historical

xi

Society of Wisconsin, Debra Anderson of the University of Wisconsin–Green Bay, and William Paul of the University of Wisconsin–Stevens Point provided valuable assistance in locating material. Denise Ready and Charmaine Harbort aided us by transcribing the original letters. Paul Hass's expert editorial advice was essential in our efforts to turn our manuscript into a book. H. Nicholas Muller III, Robert Thomasgard, and Peter Gottlieb expressed confidence in the project when it was merely an idea. Thanks are also due to John Kaminski, who served as a sounding board for the original concept of the series and whose work in documentary editing and encouragement have been an inspiration.

LETTERS
FROM THE
FRONT
1898 – 1945

1

The Spanish-American War

"Our victory was complete": Cuba

On February 15, 1898, the battleship *Maine* sank to the bottom of Havana harbor. Although it remains unclear whether the explosion aboard the *Maine* was the result of foul play, within three months a state of war existed between Spain and the United States. Rear Admiral William T. Sampson and his North Atlantic Squadron steamed down to blockade the coast of Cuba in April of that year. The assembled battleships, armored cruisers, monitors, and torpedo boats waited for the Spanish fleet under Admiral Pascual Cervera y Topete to emerge from the port of Santiago de Cuba on the southeastern shore of the island. In late June an expeditionary force of about 18,000 soldiers under General W. Rufus Shafter landed eighteen miles east of Santiago at Daiquiri.

Shafter and his men moved slowly toward Santiago, while Sampson stalked the Spanish fleet. The fighting was fierce at times, and the overland capture of the city came at the cost of about 1,500 American and 700 Spanish casualties. The decisive blow to the Spanish forces in Cuba occurred on July 3, 1898, when Cervera's fleet attempted to break out of the naval blockade. The ensuing battle ended in the destruction of the Spanish warships, the death of more than 500 Spanish sailors, and the capture of Admiral Cervera.

One young eyewitness to the naval campaign in the Caribbean survived to embark on a distinguished career with the U.S. Navy. Nathan Crook Twining was born in Boscobel in southwestern Wisconsin in 1869. An 1889 graduate of the U.S. Naval Academy, Twining was a lieutenant, junior grade, aboard the U.S.S. *Iowa* at the outbreak of the Spanish-American War. While serving on the *Iowa*, the young lieutenant witnessed the bombardment of San Juan, Puerto Rico, and fought during the destruction of the Spanish fleet at Santiago de Cuba. Twining's later naval career included service as a faculty member at the Naval War College, a Distinguished Service Medal for World War I service, and command of the U.S.S. *Texas*. He died in 1924 in Nantucket, Massachusetts, three years after his promotion to admiral.

Key West, Florida
April 12, 1898

Dear Brother: —

. . . The Spanish war still drags on and we are waiting for developments; The President's message[1] went in yesterday but we don't know yet what Congress will do about it; I should not be surprised now to see Spain throw up the sponge without a fight; if she doesn't, our first move will probably be a demonstration in force before Havana and probably a bombardment; if that doesn't have the desired effect a blockade will probably be established. That will mean two or three months of idleness and waiting, but *must* end in the surrender of the island, as we can maintain a blockade so effective that not a scrap of food can get into the island, and there is hardly two weeks' supply for the Spanish army there even we believe. The chances of a naval scrap are poor, as the enemy has nothing over here for fight with.

Tomorrow may bring peace or war — we are prepared for either.

Love to all the family,

Your brother
N C Twining

Off the Coast of Cuba
May 15, 1898

Dear Brother:

I would like to have the theatre of war shifted to a more northern climate — perhaps Greenland would be a more desirable country to scrap about at this season of the year than Cuba; the weather is something frightful, the heat and moisture combining to keep everybody in a chronic state of *sweat* — perspiration is too mild a word.

Of course the newspapers have already given you an account of the bombardment of San Juan on Thursday and you know as much about it as I do; The papers usually get all there is and generally more . . . .

Your brother
N C Twining

[1] On April 11, 1898, President William McKinley asked Congress for power to use military forces to "secure a full and final termination of hostilities between the government of Spain and the people of Cuba." Congress declared war on April 25, 1898.

WHi(X3)47076

The battleship Oregon *off the coast of Santiago de Cuba. This photograph was taken shortly after the battle described in Twining's letter of July 4, 1898.*

Off Santiago de Cuba
July 4, 1898

Dear Brother: —

Yesterday was *our* day, for which we have waited so many weary weeks. The newspapers have, of course, already told of the engagement with the Spanish fleet, and before this reaches you, all the details will have been printed.

I saw very little of the action personally, being shut up in my turret on the disengaged side, and, much to my disgust I had no chance to fire a shot, though I had to remain at my post, hoping that some good luck would bring the enemy into my field of vision.

Briefly, the facts are as follows:

About 9:30 A.M. our crew was at quarters for inspection, and the Executive [Officer] was inspecting the ship and crew, when the look-outs sighted smoke in the harbor, and immediately after a ship's bow appeared around the western point of the channel. The electric bells and bugles at once sounded to general quarters and in less than three minutes we were ready. In a few minutes more, all the Spanish ships were in sight steaming out of the channel in column at close distance. This ship was the first to open fire and for 56 minutes the firing was incessant.

The Oquendo, Maria Theresa, and two destroyers were knocked out in that time, and as nothing else was then within range of us we ceased firing.

The Spaniards had attempted to escape to the westward, but the two ships and the destroyers mentioned suffered so under the fire of this ship and the Oregon that they tried to put back to Santiago; they were in flames and were being so terribly pounded and raked that they coudn't get back but were run on the beach about 8 miles from Santiago, and surrendered there.

The Colon and Vizcaya kept on to the westward with the Brooklyn ahead of them but off shore, the Oregon and Texas hot on their trail and the Iowa bringing up the rear. In the course of 15 minutes the Vizcaya could stand it no longer and headed for the beach and hauled down her flag. We stopped to rescue survivors from her as we saw that we could not hope to come up with the Colon which was, besides, amply cared for by the Brooklyn, Oregon, and Texas. They came up with her and captured her at 1:15, about 50 miles west of Santiago.

I was sent in to bring off survivors from the Vizcaya and succeeded in getting about 200; some 200 more had reached the beach in the one boat they had and by swimming. About 100 men, including six officers, were killed on board or drowned. I picked up four drowned men whom I was unable to resuscitate; one of them was badly wounded and was probably dead when he reached the water.

The losses on the other ships were probably about the same though we haven't heard from all the rescuing ships yet. We have Admiral Cervera, Captain Eulate (of the Vizcaya), 30 officers and 240 men aboard us, whom we are to transfer to the St. Louis this afternoon. Thirty nine of the officers and men we saved were wounded, some very badly. One man died almost as soon as we got him on board, and several others will hardly survive the necessary operations and amputations.

The casualties on our side amounted, so far as reported, to one killed and two wounded, all on the Brooklyn. This ship was struck several times but nobody was hurt.

Our victory was complete and overwhelming and was won at practically no cost to ourselves. Two of our ships, the Massachusetts, and the New York, were temporarily absent, while the Indiana is so badly crippled by weak boilers that she was not able to participate in the action except at the very first; she could not pursue. The Iowa and Oregon did most of the work on the Oquendo, and Maria Teresa, with a little assistance from the Texas; the Vizcaya surrendered to this ship, while the Oregon and Brooklyn ran down and captured the Colon.

We were especially glad that the Spaniards took yesterday to come out, as our victory gives additional zest to the celebration of the 4th of July at home.

What will happen next we do not know; the Army is nearly in Santiago and has summoned the city to surrender; whether it does or not, we shall have it in a few days, as the Army can undoubtedly take it, though at the expense of a good many lives. Many of the Spanish officers think that our victory and the fall of Santiago will end the war; if not, I suppose Porto Rico will be our next point of attack. Now that the Spanish fleet is disposed of, with the exception of a couple of broken down destroyers, the Army will have to do the rest, and I hope they'll do it soon.

It is so frightfully hot down here that everybody is anxious to finish up and go home.

Incidentally, I suppose our victory of yesterday will give us about $250,000 prize money to be divided among the ships participating. It will take my share of it to replace the clothes I gave the Spanish officers, most of whom came aboard in scanty attire.

It is too hot to do anything, and I am pretty well used up after yesterday's work, so I will postpone further details until another time.

Your brother,
N C Twining

"We had a good home and we left"

Many veterans of the Spanish-American War never saw a shot fired in anger. Although the United States raised an army of more than 125,000 men in 1898, the invasion force sent to Cuba and Puerto Rico numbered only about 18,000. Wisconsin raised four regiments totalling about 3,000 men, but two of these regiments never left the country. Corporal Glenn W. Garlock (Company B, 1st Regiment, attached to the U.S. Army 7th Corps) was one of the 1,500 Wisconsin soldiers to spend the entire time in training camp. Born in Fort Atkinson in 1877, Garlock enlisted in the National Guard at age eighteen. He remained a member of the Wisconsin

Guard for twenty-four years and eventually fought with the 32nd Division as a lieutenant colonel during World War I. Beginning in 1919, Garlock worked as the editor of the *West Salem Nonpareil Journal*, a position he retained until his death in 1939.

   Garlock's letters to his parents illustrate the frustration and boredom felt by many soldiers stuck in the hot, cramped, and disease-ridden army camps in Jacksonville, Florida. Garlock once joked to his parents, "Why is the 7th Army Corp like the seat of a man's pants?" "It is never intended for the front."

Jacksonville, Florida

June 25, 1898

Dear Folks at Home; —

   All the boxes sent received in good shape and was very glad to receive them and enjoyed all the stuff very much. Am much obliged for the pins and needles, the thread and bandage, the pocket book

Army encampment in Port Tampa, Florida, c. 1898.

WHi(X3)19133

and socks and the whole shooting match, they will all come handy. As for the medicine, I don't know what I will do with that yet.

Our recruits came this morning, we all met them and shouted, we had a good home and we left, we are going to feed them on hard tack and sowbelly for a few days to break them in.

Things begin to get a little stale here. Orders and officers are more strict, we are not even allowed to wear suspenders without wearing coats, drills are harder and longer and it looks as if we would stay here all summer. For my part I like being a soldier all right but this loafing around in a camp like this with 9 or 10 thousand men around you ain't what its cracked up to be and I wished that we would commence business right away or else get a vacation. . .

Glenn

Camp Cuba Libre
Jacksonville, Florida
August 12, 1898

Dear Folks;

. . . Don't worry about my not having many luxuries. I dare say that we fare as well as lots of people up that way. Yesterday for dinner we had beef soup with lots of rice in it, besides potatoes, bread and coffee, last night we had potatoes, beef steak, fried on-ions, bread, coffee and sliced onions in vinegar if we wished to fix them up for ourselves. We have fresh beef every day, have rolled oats once a week, cabbage once in a while so that we won't starve by any means. I weigh 145 lbs, which shows how little an impression hardtack and sowbelly has made on me. . . .

Do not think I will inlist in the regulars after the war is over as they would not take me on account of my teeth. Anyway I have had just about enough of this life. I don't want to do garrison duty any-where, this is monotonous enough. I inlisted to fight and not to lay around some southern sand field and catch the malaria. It seems too bad that the troops of this command should lay around this camp all summer and never a regt in the whole division has gone to the front. Should a strong force be required to garrison the island of Cuba or any of the other new possessions of the U.S. it will proba-bly be our luck to be called on, no one can tell anything about it. However the less we worry about it the better. . . .

Goodbye,
Glenn Garlock

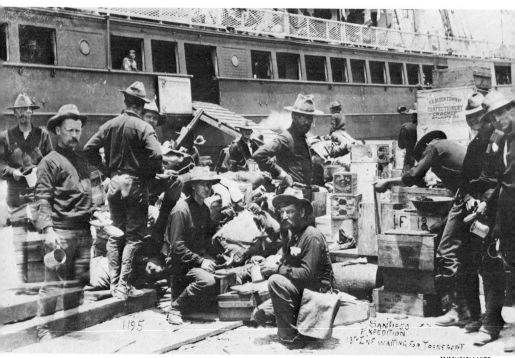

WHi(X3)11072

Thirteenth U.S. Infantry embarking for the invasion of Cuba, 1898.

Camp Cuba Libre
Jacksonville, Florida
August 23, 1898

Dear People:

How are you all taking my sickness, not worrying I hope. You got my letter written Sunday didn't you. It does not seem a very serious case, the fever was at 100 3/5 this morning, it has gone down about 2/5 of a degree every day. I have had to take no ice baths as do those who have a high fever. I hope to be convelesent in about two week, will then be sent to Pablo Beach[2] to rest and recuperate on sea breezes. Will be pretty weak then cause all I have for nourishment is a small amount of milk, am not very weak yet, will write you as often and as long as I can. It gets pretty tiresome laying around all day. Do not sleep very well cause I rest so much.

---

[2] A small beach on the outkirts of Jacksonville.

They give me two big quinine[3] pills three times a day. I call them cannon balls. There is a nice looking lady nurse taking care of one of the very sick patients. The rest of the fellows hardly know whether to vote her a nuisance or not, they don't like to call for pots etc when she is around allthough they are supposed to just the same. Besides quinine I get a capsule with turpentine in to swallow. Charles Ives is pretty sick. Our company has a very large number in the Hospital. It had been very well but I guess its turn has come. I suppose you live on game from John's rifle now. Are you a pretty good shot Howie? I must confess my rifle brings me rather a slim living. I will get out in time to strengthen up and go to Cuba. It is decided that the 7th Corp, will go to Cuba and I am shure Col. Shadel has decided to go, and only the most powerful influence will hold me back. Well good bye

Glenn

"Viva Americano seemed to be the watchword": Puerto Rico

The United States invaded the island of Puerto Rico on July 21, 1898, with a force of 3,314 soldiers. At first, the Spanish garrison there offered little resistance, and local residents welcomed the American troops. Wisconsin volunteers finally received their first taste of battle in the war when they captured Coamo, a small town in the interior of Puerto Rico. On August 9, 1898, the 2nd and 3rd regiments advanced under fire toward the Spanish garrison at Coamo and drove the Spanish into an ambush by Pennsylvania troops. One soldier who participated in the fight was Edward C. Niebuhr of Wausau, Wisconsin. Niebuhr marched with Company G in the 3rd Regiment and wrote to his cousin soon after the skirmish at Coamo.

Coamo Battlefield, Puerto Rico
August 19, 1898

Dear Cousin, —
I received your letter at Charleston, S.C. Now I am nearly 1,500 miles from there on the beautiful island of Porto Rico. All kinds of tropical fruits grow there in the rich soil. The farms around here are not worked. The Spanish soldiers used to take all the [*torn*] as soon as they were [*torn*] and so the natives quit working them.
The Spaniards treated the natives most shamefully. They took anything they wanted from the natives without paying for it. They

[3] Physicians during the Spanish-American War used quinine pills, a popular remedy for fever and pain, to combat the symptoms of malaria.

did not allow the natives to go to school or church. Schools and churches are for the Spanish aristocrats. The priests will have nothing to do with the natives. They will not baptize them, marry them, or burry them and yet the priests call themselves Christians.

When we first landed on the island the natives thought we would do as the Spanish soldiers did; rob and plunder. They gave us cigars, cigaretts and fruits to keep on the right side of us but when they found out that we had money and had to pay for every thing we wanted, and were not allowed to steal they began to charge high prices for thier wares.

We took possession of Ponce, a city of 38,000 inhabitants, without a skirmish. This disappointed us greatly as we expected a fight and were prepared for it. We each carried 100 rounds of ammunition, two days' rations, and a small package of bandages for wounds.

Shortly after we landed, we were given Crag-Jorgensen rifles in place of the old Springfields. These new guns are dandies. They

American soldiers in Cuba writing home.
WHi(X3)14274

shoot steel capped bullets that will kill at two miles. They use smokeless powder and have a magazine of 5 shells. Single shell can also be fired. The bullet is 30 caliber. The Span[ish] use the Mauser rifle, a gun similar to ours, shoots a 28 caliber bullet.

On Aug 7th we marched about twenty miles into the interior and camped for the night. The next day we marched a few miles farther, within two miles of a Spanish blockhouse and intrenchment and stayed there for the night. At 7 o'clock on the morning of Aug 9th our artilery opeaned fire upon the blockhouse, blew it up and drove the Spanish from thier intrenchments. This was the beginning of the Battle of Coamo. The 1st Brigade, consisting of the 2nd & 3rd Wis. and the 16th Penn. followed the Spanish troops up, cornered them a few miles up the road, killed 8 or 10 and wounded from 40 to 50 Spaniards and never lost an man and only a few wounded. The 16th Penn. did all the shooting and claim all the glory, but the Wisconsin boys are entitled to thier share of it. They did as much dangerous work, being under fire several times but were not allowed to fire.

On the 12th of August the report was around camp that peace had been concluded but when we heard the cannon roar for eight hours during the day a few miles up the valley, we did not put much faith in the report. My company was on outpost and picket duty that day so I wasn't in that fight. Two men from Co. L., 3d Wis. from Sparta were killed by an exploding shell. [*torn*] first and only lives [of] Americans lost in battle in Porto Rico that I know of.

On the 13th of Aug. Pres Mc Kinley sent a message ordering us to cease hostilities and now we have quit fighting and are camped on the site of the Battle of Coamo. I do not know when we are going home.

Your cousin
Ed

"The boys are dieing off very fast"

Sickness quickly tarnished the glory of battle for Wisconsin soldiers serving in Puerto Rico. Immediately following the victory at Coamo, malaria and dysentery ravaged the troops, resulting in sixty-four deaths and hospitalizing almost half the 2,000 men in the 2nd and 3rd regiments. During the course of the entire war, over two thousand American men died of disease, compared to the 385 killed in action. Unfortunately, these casualties rarely made front-page news in an American press hungry for military heroics and colonial splendor. As one Wisconsin soldier wrote home, "You don't know half of what's going on down here, or in other words,

not half has ever been told." (La Crosse *Daily Republican and Leader,* September 26, 1898.)
La Crosse's own Company M of the 3rd Regiment tried to relate the suffering and misery of army life in Puerto Rico in a letter written to Frank Van Meter, city editor of the La Crosse *Daily Republican and Leader.* Although this particular letter was never published, similar petitions were sent to newspapers all over Wisconsin from units anxious to return home. One letter from La Crosse soldiers yearning to leave Puerto Rico drew the ire of the editor of the *La Crosse Morning Chronicle.* "However much one sympathizes with the soldiers' anxiety to go home now that the war is over," the *Chronicle* wrote, "there is no doubt that the general attitude has been most unreasonable" (September 11, 1898). Company M and the rest of the 3rd Regiment finally left their encampment on October 12, 1898, and arrived back in the United States eight days later.

Puerto Rico
September 12, 1898

Friend Frank: —

As the boys of Co. M. wanted all their friends to know the hardships we are suffering here in Porto Rico and to have it put in all the LaCrosse Papers we all thought you would be the right person to write to so we take the pleasure to do it and we hope it will touch the hearts of the people enough so they will look into the matter and find out if we have to stay here the two years or if we can reach home this fall before we are all dead as the boys are dieing off very fast and out of our regiment we have got four hundred sick with fever in the division hospital and we see every day more men taken out of the Regiment, we have seen twelve buried last week and three more died last night and three of the Sparta boys cannot last over twenty four hours. The Doctor says it is a sad sight to gaze on the tents crowded with sick and dieing and the chief surgeon of the expidition said the boys were so far from the North that they could not stand the heat and if we were to stay here for any length of time and the boys were taken away as fast as they are now we would all be in the hospital in thirty days more. We got up a petition stating we would all like to return to the states because they have got lots of regulars here to do garrison duty here and it had to first pass through Col. Moores hands and one of the boys said that when he read it he said Oh hell this is not military at all and he tore it up, that shows what kind of a Col we have got. He draws more money here than he does pulling teeth in LaCrosse so he wants us all to stay but we will try hard to get away. Now if you people there can imagine what misery we are in and you ought to see the rotten pork and tomatoes we have to eat, only sometimes we go over the mountains and have to kill some poor natives chickens or calf which are very scarce and we if caught doing it would be court-martialed. And it is very [un]pleasant. B. Blanchard and Ray Hiscox borrowed each a red cross, pinned them on their arm and passed through the guardlines to get up town to buy something to eat and to buy a pair of native shoes and they were caught by the city provost guards and sent to Col. Moore and he court martialed them and they got five days each in the guard house at heavy duty; a[i]nt that hell. First they tell us we will move in a few days and get the boys all excited, then when the day comes they say a few days longer. We are camped right where we had our first fight the ninth of August[4] and it is getting to be worse every day. If we ever live to reach LaCrosse we can tell stories of hardships that would cause many a tear to flow and now we hope the many friends of the soldier boys of LaCrosse will push this thing along and if they know of any good news concerning our coming home we would be very pleased to hear it right away as we have almost given up all hopes of ever returning home alive again. That fever works on the strongest men the hardest so the Doctors say. Co. M. has only got fourteen men able to do light duty out of one hundred and six strong and robust men when they left their homes (are dead) and Co. B. has got twenty two for light duty all the rest of the boys are in the hospital except just a few that would not be taken there and they lay in their tents unable to walk around and you see the well ones have got to do all the fatigue duty and all the guard duty so they will soon all be run down and sick and it wont be many days either. Poor Shattuck,[5] old boy, has got more than he can tend to in the drug department and sitting up even at night with the sick ones in our company and giving them alchol baths. We would be lost if anything should happen to the old boy so we hope he wont get sick. We were told this morning that one of the boys out of the sixteenth Penn. Regt now in the hospital was to be bathed yesterday afternoon and his comrades went over to do it and he undressed him and washed his legs and he did not have life enough to stir around and when his comrade raised his arms to wash under them he was surprised to find that the maggots had began to eat in his flesh and the doctor cut them out from under each arm but they say he has got to die. Isn't that an awful thing. It

---

[4] The battle of Coamo, described in Edward Niebuhr's letter printed above.
[5] Charles E. Shadduck, assistant hospital steward of the 3rd Regimental Staff. Shadduck wrote to a friend five days later, "We are still on the island and in bad shape. . . . Of late we have been losing one or two men a day."

was all on account of not getting no care because they have got so many to look after and the nurses are our own boys. They do not know how to care for the sick but they do every thing they can for the poor sick ones so you can just imagine a very little of how we are situated in this death centre of the globe. So now we hope you will please state this news to the papers. Frank you will do us a great favor indeed and if we ever return we will reward you for your kindness. The report was just this minute given out by the Regimental clerk that out of thirteen hundred soldiers in camp when we came only three hundred and sixty are now able for light duty. So this is all I will have time to tell about this time and shall wait to see this in print in one of the LaCrosse papers which I know you will put this in. I will close for this time and hoping to hear from you friends from home. Any one of your boys letters will be gladly received and please send us the latest paper clippings concerning our coming home this fall. We do not hear any news very often. Well I will stop. When you write send all of the letters to Ed Shattuck as he is always here in camp when we are out on six days guard. Now please do not

Army field hospital, Cuba, 1898.

WHi(X3)47087

overlook this and publish immediately so good bye. From your friends of the gallant Co. M. or what there is left of us.

The War in the Pacific

Commodore George Dewey's crushing victory over the Spanish fleet at Manila Bay on May 1, 1898, represented only the beginning of American military involvement in the Philippines. Although an indigenous independence movement had existed for years, the Spanish surrendered to American forces in August, 1898, rather than recognize the newly proclaimed Philippine Republic. An uneasy peace existed between American authorities and the Philippine resistance until February 4, 1899, when open warfare broke out. Until his capture in 1901, Emilio Aguinaldo led the Philippine nationalists in a guerilla campaign against the United States. More than 100,000 American troops fought against Aguinaldo's Insurrectos in brutal jungle campaigns until the last vestiges of resistance were crushed in the spring of 1902.

Charles King (1844 –1933) of Milwaukee was graduated from West Point in 1866 and spent the next decade fighting frontier campaigns against the Apache, Sioux, Cheyenne, and Nez Percé Indians. In 1880 King returned to Wisconsin to serve as the University of Wisconsin's military professor. Two years later, he became the Wisconsin National Guard's chief instructor, and from 1895 to 1897 he served as adjutant general of Wisconsin.

When war broke out, King accepted a commission as a brigadier general of the U.S. Volunteers. He briefly served as commanding general of the Department of Hawaii and later commanded the 1st Brigade of the 1st Division in the Philippines. One private described him as "immaculately attired and calmly lighting a cigar, although the bullets were whizzing around in a most reckless manner." After the war, King returned to St. John's Military Academy in Delafield, Wisconsin, where he taught until 1931. King was also a prolific writer of military fiction, with fifty-two novels and approximately 200 short stories to his name. The following letters to his daughter, Carol, provide an intimate picture of King's service overseas.

Honolulu, Hawaii
October 20, 1898

. . . Not only has my heart been wrung on their account and the nights have been sleepless and the days harrowing, but here, too, my poor boys far from their home are stricken down by scores with fever that has already carried off five and others are at death's door. Our big hospital is overcrowded — our doctors overworked — our nurses inadequate and the conditions grow daily worse. Two of my young physicians have broken down entirely and the Chief Surgeon has just told me he thought that one of them could not pull through.

. . . The Filipinos promise to keep us busy all Winter & Spring. Troops will not be mustered out there for a good while and — if my orders are not again countermanded, I hope to see varied & stirring service there. The Arizona — unluckily, went to Hong Kong and cannot get to us now before the 26th by which time another mail comes from the States & another chance of days disappointment.

Meantime we are overwhelmed with work and perplexities. There is little time now for social entertainments & I have no heart for them — having declined all invitations for a fortnight back. There are a thousand cares & responsibilities pressing upon me and I heartily wish we had never been ordered here to Honolulu. . . .

Devotedly, dear Carol
Your own Daddy

WHi(X3)39260
General Charles King, c. 1900.

Convalescent Hospital
South Manila, Philippines[6]
December 18, 1898

. . . Somehow I cannot feel that this is to be a Merry Christmas for any of us. I am still far too anxious about you all and, as for myself, tho' I have at last reached the field of possible active service and am where I have long wished to be — I find the condition of affairs most unsatisfactory to almost any officer with whom I have talked — from the Commanding General[7] down. The unsettled treaty of peace over which our Senate may debate for months. The feeling of the Insurgents that they are being robbed by the Americans of the fruits of all their victories and all their really brave efforts to free the islands from the tyranny of Spain; the active & insidious efforts of the Spanish priesthood & the German residents[8] to stir up trouble between us & the Filipinos all point to a clash in the near future & only consummate coolness & mutual courtesy & patience will prevent it. The air is full of rumors & alarms. The Filipinos have been lead to believe we are preparing to attack them & so have thrown up earthworks and planted cannon commanding the approaches to the outlying villages they occupy. The Americans have been warned that there is to be a great local uprising of the natives within our lines some still might — in conjunction with an attack in force from without & that the American officers are to be murdered in their beds (The Fillies will have some lively experiences when they try that game), and so, as mere precautions we have had to strengthen our outposts. Though not yet sufficiently recovered to ride or walk except a few rods[9] at a time I reported for duty three days ago & since then have spent much time rearranging my "front" which *at present*, as you will see by the map I sent Ruf[10] is from Blockhouse 12 to the Pasig in front of Pandácan — the three

---

[6] Shortly after his arrival in Manila, King contracted a severe case of eczema, from an infected vaccination. He spent most of November and December recuperating.

[7] Major General Elwell S. Otis commanded the U.S. forces in the Philipine Islands from August 29, 1898, to May 5, 1900.

[8] Kaiser Wilhelm II of Germany believed that the Philippines would be a valuable overseas asset for his country and sent a squadron of German cruisers to Manila Bay soon after Dewey's victory.

[9] A rod equals approximately 16.5 feet.

[10] Rufus King, Charles's son and namesake of Milwaukee's Civil War General Rufus King (1814–1876).

villages of Paca, Peirà, Francia, & Pandácan being just inside my lines & the Insurgents being in force at Sta. Ana a mile away. . . .

Devotedly Your Own Daddy

Manila, Philippines
January 31, 1899

You will not make a wry face at this wrinkled paper, my own dear Brownie, when I tell you that it is almost the best Daddy has just now — and pretty or suitable stationery seems hard to get here. In a little over an hour he must be off — looking over the lines again and all to-night he must spend at the front — and lots of other nights apparently, for we are constantly being ordered to exercise the greatest vigilance — to guard against attack etc. and I dare say these little Filipinos think they've got the Yankees scared half crazy — when the fact is it is getting to be hard work to keep our own tempers and our men from rushing the Insurgent lines and eating them up. Immunity from punishment for all manner of little pieces of impudence or aggression had made them very bold — but you see we have been restrained by orders from home on *no* account to get into conflict with them — and last night the war was almost begun right in my own brigade — a company of Idaho volunteers came within an ace of marching slap thro the lines & that would almost assuredly have brought on a battle. Things cannot go on this way very much longer and now the belief is that the Insurgent Cabinet[11] will order an attack within the next week but I fear they wont. . . .

Your devoted *Daddy*

Like many American soldiers, Martin Stuhr (Company L, 18th U.S. Volunteers) briefly stopped in the Hawaiian Islands on the way to the Philippines. In 1893, American-led insurgents overthrew Queen Liliuokalani and established an independent republic in 1894. During the summer of 1898, the United States formally annexed Hawaii, and it became a U.S. territory in 1900. Stuhr's letter, written to N. C. Ward, provides an example of how America's recent acquisitions in the Pacific must have appeared to Wisconsin soldiers fighting overseas.

[11] Soon after the treaty between the United States and Spain, Aguinaldo formed a government representing an independent Philippine republic.

Jaro Hospital
Iloilo, Philippines
August 16, 1899

Dear Sir,

Many days, weeks, and months have passed away since I left the Healthy Climate of California, and sailed through the Golden Gate to the land beyond the Seas, ever will I remember the feeling and Sensation that passed over both Officers and men alike when they stood on deck of transport, on the bright and sunny afternoon as we saw our native land wherein dweldt our Folks & Friends and Loved ones Slowly Pass out of Sight. but it was not for long for Suddenly something way down in the Stomack seemed to demand our atention and one or the other would be seen leaning over the rail at the same bringing action into words (Heave up), which lasted about 24 hours. on the 4 day we passed the Leprosy Island,[12] and on the 5th we sighted ohau Island. The morning of the 6 day we lay in Harbor of Honolulu, and when the sun send its first rays across the sea its light fell on and developed a scene so Beautiful and Grand, that I with my poor learning and training will not try and describe it. we had reached the Hawaian Island and a Paradise it seemed, true to its name, we landed the next day and remained long enough to see the Stars and Stripes waveing Proudly in the Breezes and over Americas new born Infantry. we made a tour of the Island and Visited an Extinct Volcano known as Diamond Head, Punch bowl, Pearl City. The Coffee and Sugar Plantation and also the famous and Historical Pali Pass. we were given a reception at the Ex-Queen Palace and had the pleasure of seeing her and the Princess Personaly, Also President Dole[13] and others. we had a pleasant time, and almost regreted to leave when a few days later we receaved orders to leave.

After 16 days more sailing we entered the Harbor of Manila and soon came with in sight of wrecks and ruins of the Spanish Boats,[14] and in a Short time Passed and Anchored besides the fleet that had Struck such a powerful blow on May 1st 98.

remaining their untill Xmas Eve 24 Dec. we embarked and sailed for Iloilo 350 miles South of Manila, but did not Land untill the 10. of Feb. and from that time untill now we have had all kinds of times

[12] The Hawaiian island of Molokai housed a leper colony and was commonly known as Leprosy Island.

[13] Sanford Ballard Dole (1844–1926) was President of the Republic of Hawaii (1894–1898) and later became the first governor of the territory of Hawaii.

[14] The twelve burned-out hulls of the Spanish Pacific fleet destroyed by Admiral Dewey and the U.S. Asiatic Squadron during the battle of Manila Bay (May 1, 1898).

and many very many have been laid away beneath the sod and it is my Candid opinion that even with 100,000 men it will take another year at least before they the Insurgents will surrender.

at present we have only a foot-hold, and may say just began. This is no white mans Country. out of 30,000 troops 6,000 are now in Hospital, not Including 1,500 wounded. and about 40 percent of the men are a physical wreck, fever, Dysentary, Small Pox, and Native Diseases of all kinds.

with a little Capital a man can make money here. plenty of opertunitys, but Everything is as yet uncertain. There are 10 natives to 1 Soldier in town and if they have the Courage the Entire City will go up in Smoke Some day and *Otis* is to blame. he is M[ajor] G[eneral].

I have a large number of news here Consisting of Bombardment of Iloilo.[15] The Landing of our Troops under fire. the burning of the City, the old Forts, the Insurgent Army. Etc. also a number of Relics and Curios but am afraid they will get lost if I Send them, but if I live will be home by Xmas, at least Expect to be, as most of us are in the shape of a Spanish Battle Ship, and should I arrive you may have my Collection for Exhibit and now Trusting and Hopeing you and yours are well and Happy, and Trusting we may have a friendly Toot together when the days of war are over.

With Best Love and Wishes to from your friend and Soldier

Martin Stuhr

The Philippine campaign was marked by war atrocities committed by all sides. The insurgent tactics of dismemberment, torture, and killing of prisoners were often met with chillingly similar responses from American soldiers. Commonly held attitudes about white racial superiority only served to further justify inhuman cruelty. For every wounded Filipino soldier, fifteen were killed — a statistic that suggests the vicious nature of combat in which American soldiers rarely took prisoners.

William "Billy" Mitchell (1879 –1934) was one eyewitness to this kind of warfare. Mitchell came from a prominent Milwaukee family and enlisted in the U.S. Army at age eighteen. He briefly served in Wisconsin's 1st Regiment in Florida and Cuba during the Spanish-American War before his promotion to second lieutenant and transfer to the Philippines. Mitchell campaigned with General Arthur MacArthur in northern Luzon throughout the Insurrection, and his letters to his uncle and mother reveal the strong racial undertones that marked warfare in "the bush." A career soldier, Mitchell served with the Army Air Corps in France during World War I and is widely recognized as one of America's pioneers in air power

[15] A port city on the island of Panay nearly 300 miles south of Manila. After languishing outside the city for six weeks, American forces captured Iloilo from the insurgents in February, 1899.

doctrine. Outspoken and controversial, Mitchell resigned as a general in
the Army following his court-martial for insubordination in 1925.

Bautista, Philippines
December 14, 1899

My dear Uncle Doc

. . . Well, we have been keeping still for the last few days and are
beginning to get rather restless but guess that I shall soon be ac-
comodated with all the advancing I can take care of. I am now act-
ing as chief signal officer of Gen. McArthurs[16] division, dont know
how long I shall be but probably for several weeks. We have these
Gugus[17] pretty well on the run now and they are breaking up into
small bands, which we have to chase around the country. The last
scrap we had with the whole division was at Bamban,[18] where we
soon routed them. I got some good shots in there with my carbine at
250 yds. range and could pick my men they were so near. However,
we have not been skinning any Phillipinos as yet but some of them
need it badly enough. They are a very funny people from our point
of view as stoical as our indians. Utterly unmindful of pain or intense feeling if their outward appearance counts for anything. The
climate here is my ideal of what a climate should be. Cool mornings
warm in the middle of the day to be sure Cool evenings and very
cold nights. I enclose a newspaper picture & clipping. It is a very
good one as we used this kind of transportation along the Manila
Dagupau railroad where the track was in tack, but instead of being
behind the line we are nearly always in front of it.

I never enjoyed better health. Have more flesh then I had in Milwaukee and seem to be able to stand most any old thing. We have
come through rice fields with water up to ones waist, through
woods thickets of bamboo, across rivers with currents like a mill
race where men drown instantly, if they are washed off rafts or lose
their hold of ropes we stretch across and all this right in the face of
these insurrectos who are well armed apparently well officered and
with plenty of ammunition but pitifully incompetent in marksmanship. They don't seem to kill such a great many of us considering
the amount of ammunition they use. This is a fine country and a
desirable place for the U.S. to hold in my opinion for many reasons,

[16] Arthur MacArthur (1845–1912), a career military officer, had served with the 24th
Wisconsin Volunteer Infantry during the Civil War and held the position of military governor of the Philippines (1900–1901). He was the father of General Douglas MacArthur.
[17] A racial epithet used by American troops to describe Filipinos. The name originally
comes from the tree bark used as shampoo by some Filipino women.
[18] A small town on the island of Luzon about fifty miles northwest of Manila.

which you know probably much better then I. . . . Am enjoying this very much. Have good ponies men who will follow me anywhere and are good shots, good telegraph operators, good cooks and good everything the best scouts in the business also. . . .

I remain As Ever
Wm. Mitchell

Capas, Philippines
January 7, 1900

My dear Uncle Doc
. . . Have been fairly busy this week building lines to different places. But we will have a little rest soon I guess. It does not make much difference with me however as this kind of work just agrees with me. Got a few days hunting deer and boars. We hunt them on horseback with lances and pistols. Have had Negritos as brush beaters. They are the aborigines you know are about 4 feet high and

"Don't think they will capture me alive at this stage of the game if I am armed." American troops man the front lines in the Philippines.
WHi(X3)6033

resemble the Africans in other particulars. They wear no clothes to speak of except a string around their waists in which they carry knives. They use bows and arrows and lances. They are good hunters too. These Gugus lined five men of one infantry regiment up against a fence shot and cut them up as we were entering a town. We took no prisoners after that. This was in a place called Arryot. Don't think they will capture me alive at this stage of the game if I am armed. Sometimes one cannot help it. They are getting pretty desperate now. . . .

I remain Yours Truly
Wm. Mitchell

Manila, Philippines
January 25, 1900

My dear Mother

We have been having quite a little rain lately considering this to be the dry season. But in volume of course it does not compare to the rain fall in the wet season. Have been in town here about two weeks in Command of the Company and am trying to get some of Capt. Carr's property in shape. It is pretty badly mixed as everyone else's is. This is the first chance I have had of seeing Manila as I was here only a day or two when I arrived. Our troops are all over Luzon now and they are gradually going all over the other islands. They have extended the curfew hour to ten oclock in the night now instead of half past light. There are a great many American ladies here now. When I first came, It was not considered safe for them to be around. Aguinaldo's whereabouts are a mystery to us although the secret service undoubtedly know where he is. It will be quite a question for us to decide if we should get him as to what to do with him. I think that what little insurrection in an organized way, if there still is such a thing, will go on in the same way without him. The best way would be to quietly shoot him or kill him and get him out of the way. This would occasion no howl in the States and the Gugus would soon find out that he was gone for good. Col. Moxfield is in town now. Drove around the Luneta[19] and took supper with him yesterday. There is a good deal of talk that Gen. Mc-Arthur will supercede Gen. Otis as Military Governor here. Gen. Otis will probably stay until the rainy season I suppose. These Gugus will try to make up a little bit during the rainy season, no doubt and as it is very hard to carry military operations on during

[19] A large park near the center of Manila.

that time. They will be able to pick up a little. Next Winter however will see the end absolutely except for bands of marauders. The U.S. is trying to do a thing here in two years with 100 thousand men what another would do with 300 thousand in twenty. And the U.S. will come pretty near doing it. Took lunch with Col. Garlington a few days ago. He is in good health and thinks this a fine place as far as climate is concerned. Really all this talk one hears about climate is foolishness to a great extent. Here I have been in the field steadily for three months drinking out of every pool sometimes little or nothing to eat and sleeping anywhere with wet clothes or dry ones as the occasion demanded and I am all right. Of course this kind of work will tell on anyone in any climate. Have you seen anything of Mrs. Thules party yet? With love to all.

Your Affect. Son
Wm. Mitchell

2

World War I

"I am still homesick as the deuce"

On April 6, 1917, the United States entered the First World War with an army of only 125,000 men. By the close of the war, over 4 million Americans were in uniform, with roughly half this number in Europe. Army training camps were the first stop in the long process of transforming civilians into soldiers. In camps all over the United States, the 122,215 Wisconsin soldiers who served during the war learned marksmanship, military protocol, personal combat, and drill tactics. They also encountered newly developed intelligence tests designed to screen out the "feeble-minded," the War Department's ban on liquor for soldiers, and chronic shortages of both equipment and uniforms.

Harry Trippe was one "summer soldier" who eventually found a career in the Army. Born in Whitewater, Trippe (1872–1939) received a degree in civil engineering from the University of Wisconsin in 1896 and later worked for the U.S. Geological Survey, a number of private railways, the Interstate Commerce Commission, the city of Whitewater, and the port of Milwaukee. Trippe joined the Engineer Officers Reserve Corps in 1917 and the following year was sent overseas as a lieutenant colonel in command of the 308th Engineer Regiment. Trippe remained in the armed forces after the war, serving as a major in the regular army. His letters to his wife, Culla, whom he married in 1905, reveal some of the difficulties faced by soldiers in training.

Fort Leavenworth, Kansas
June 29, 1917

Dearest Girl: —
A fine day — Friday evening five thirty, and the band is playing outside my window, it is a band of prisoners and they play very well. I am still homesick as the deuce and want to be with you all — your letter today was so blue it made me worse — cheer up dear Girl, the three months will soon be up and back I come for a good old stay. No chance for me on the active list and I am beginning to

25

get glad of it. I am the old man of the company — think of it — 142 men and I am the oldest — thank Goodness they do not call me Grandpa though.

This morning six hundred of us represented Kansas Blues and six hundred Missouri Reds and we got across the river and they entrenched on the hills and we had a good time — it was interesting — most of the bunch are so weak from dysentary it is no joke. I have stopped I am happy to say — but I do not eat any meat out of the mess hall any more — I think that is what did it. Allen — my roommate — has his wife coming out to supper and bring it to him in a basket — See I wish it were you and the girls coming. Tuesday we start rifle practice in the big range and it will take most of the week — I hope I can make a good enough score to qualify but doubt it. Please try and take things easy as you can Dearest and do not worry about me — the chances are so slim of my ever being called again

*Colonel Harry Trippe and his car in Neuwied, Germany,
February 13, 1919.*

WHi(X3)47074

WHi(X3)47084

Inductees marching in training camp, c. 1917. The simplest forms of military training — such as marching in a straight line — had to be taught to American "summer soldiers" before they were issued uniforms or equipment. American Press photo.

for active service after this is over with, it is not worth considering. will have to fall in for retreat in five minutes —

Kiss the Girls

All my love

Harry

Paul W. Lappley (1894–1985) was born in the Madison suburb of Middleton. He served as a legislative page and later went to Lansing, Michigan, for training in automotive work. During the war, Lappley was a motor transport sergeant in the Ordnance Division of the Coast Artillery Corps. He contracted the Spanish flu while making the journey to France and spent the first few weeks overseas in a company hospital. After the war, Lappley returned to Madison where he opened a storage garage and served as chief deputy sheriff of Dane County. These letters to his younger brother, Walter, and his mother describe the leveling influence of army life and the attempts of the military to segregate new recruits from wounded veterans.

Camp Hancock
Augusta, Georgia
August 13, 1918
Chick [Walter Lappley],
   . . . I met some Pennsylvania boys at the Liberty theatre last nite, who have been here nine months. They are physically unfit for service and are members of the 128th Field Artillery. They were here last winter and said that two of their men froze to death on guard duty. Their regiment is fighting in France now, and they don't know what will happen to them.
   We had two high school profs in this company, one sanitary engineer and a young new york millionare. They are professional dishwashers now. We also have a Wisconsin Lawyer, who is a graduate of several Universities, he is a mailboy here. In our tent we have a fellow who studied to become a priest — after being here a month he swears as bad as the rest of us. . . .

Sincerely
Paul

Camp Stuart
Newport News, Virginia
October 1, 1918
Dear Mother,
   . . . I was vaccinated again yesterday, this makes the seventh time and they never work. They have given it up now. I took the final overseas examination today, this is the seventh one also.
   Several hundred wounded men landed here today, they came from France and wore all kinds of bandages. We were not allowed to talk to them but one fellow said to us "Boys its sure hell over there," they were all infantrymen but three. Some had to be carried on stretchers
   The regiment that is to go with us has fifty cases of Spanish influenza[1] in a single battery — so far we have none. I saw fifteen men carried to the base hospital today they all had the same thing. . . .

Paul W. Lappley

Robert Whitney of Delafield was a recruit anxious to get into the thick of things "over there." In this letter to Charles Brown, director of the State Historical Society's museum, Whitney related the excitement and anticipation that young men going off to war often displayed.

[1] During the epidemic of 1918, the U.S. Army reported more than 300,000 cases of influenza. In France, 12,000 American soldiers died from either pneumonia or the flu that year.

St. Julien's Creek, Virginia
November 5, 1918

My Dear Mr. Brown,

. . . None of us fellows here want to get out of the service with only service in U.S. to our credit. At home we may be able to feel we were in it but outside of home we're just as ready as anybody to stop and listen to a Marine from "over there" tell us about "it". There are a number of wounded ones at the hospital here and I've heard quite a bit about the life over there but one fellow said that the marines have a hard time in the fighting end but they get fine treatment and the officers will drink with them and talk in great style. From what he said they live about as different from us, over there, as we do from the civilians here. . . .

There's one thing I'm glad of every time I think of it. That is that all the time I was living at Delafield I had the freedoms of the hills and country to keep in trim on and also that Mother and Dad allowed me to fool around with the old muskets etc with which we had so much fun playing war with. I believe it has done a lot for me even if I had never had a real war to fight in. It hasn't made me a capt. or anything but I got used to the ideas of military standing. . . .

Sincerely yours,
Robert Whitney

"France at Last"

Following the ordeal of training camp, many men and women faced the new experience of crossing the Atlantic to join the American Expeditionary Force in France. The journey often began in Hoboken, New Jersey, where soldiers boarded a motley collection of old luxury liners, captured German ships, and converted freighters. During the ten-day trip, convoys of troop carriers faced threats from German U-boats (numbering about 127 subs in late 1917), but the U.S. lost only three warships to German torpedo attacks once the war began.

The relative safety of the trip did not always translate into comfort. American soldiers often described their Atlantic crossing as cramped, dirty, and noisy. Rather than putting an end to these conditions, arrival in France often saw them cramped into small boxcars intended for forty men and eight horses that took them to advanced training camps in the interior of France. The following three letters provide accounts of the journey to France and efforts to become accustomed to a foreign land.

Margaret Rowland found the Atlantic crossing exciting despite a submarine attack. Rowland grew up in Racine and studied to be a nurse before the war. With the Red Cross in France, she served in both American and French military hospitals before meeting her future husband,

John Bradley Delehanty. Rowland married Delehanty in France and eventually returned to Long Island, New York, where she worked as a nurse in local hospitals and was an avid photographer until her death at age sixty-eight in 1962.

At Sea
April 27, 1918

Dearest Family —

. . . The weather is perfect. We steamed out of New York harbor on the most beautiful day and it gave me a queer pang when I saw the dear old Statue of Liberty fading away in the distance — You never realize how thouroughly patriotic you are, and how wonder-

Margaret Rowland in France.
Courtesy Anne Geddes.
WHi(X3)47095

fully proud you are of your country, and how glad you are to be an American as when you see that marvelous New York sky line sinking into the horizon.

I was a wee bit homesick too! Oh! Papa and family — please forgive me for those last homesick, cowardly letters — I was just sort of forlorn and alone — I knew none of the nurses — and I had to attend to all of my baggage — etc. (a thing that I have almost never had to do) by myself. . . .

We have had an interesting trip. One minute you are listening to an inspiring sermon by Dr. Jowett,[2] the next trying to talk French to a French lieutenant, whose father, Richet, by the way, is a very famous sculptor. Then you find yourself talking with and listening a thrilling tale of Madame St. Clair Stobart,[3] who has been made a major in the Serbian army and who led thousands of Serbian women and children over the mountains, undergoing privations almost inconceivable. You find yourself sitting, listening, with tears pouring down your cheeks when she tells you of the horrible suffering of those absolutely expatriated Serbian people. No homes, no family, no country! Think of it! She was arrested in Belgium by the Germans and was sentenced to be shot as a spy. She escaped and was arrested again. This time, the German general said, "You are English, and whether right or wrong — *this is a war of annihilation*"! So you can see their attitude from the start. . . .

Well! little do you know of the excitement that has occured between this sentence and the last one — (Indicated by little crosses)! Even the ink in my pen has changed color! I was sitting here, writing when suddenly — the most awful quake — a thudding boom — we arose — everyone in the lounge — as one man — calmly put our life preservers — which by the way we have been carrying for days — *everywhere* — and calmly took our places by our life boats and waited for the signal. I was still carrying my fountain pen — and in a moment of extreme panic — gave it to the Japanese Count and calmly asked him to close it for me. He looked dazed and handed it back. All this very calmly. We waited — nothing happened — and nothing has happened yet. They thot they sighted a submarine and so began operations, which I cannot tell you here. It was awfully good practice. I thot of you all — and prayed a little and thanked

---

[2] John Henry Jowett (1864 –1923) was an English clergyman and inspirational writer.
[3] Stobart, an Englishwoman, was the founder and leader of two Balkan war relief societies.

my stars that I could swim. My knees are still slightly black and
blue from crashing together. . . .

All my love,
Margaret

Lieutenant Conrad M. Fox of Milwaukee (Company L, 364th Infantry)
spent the war as a white officer in command of a unit comprising only
black soldiers. Fox's letter to U.W. registrar William Hiestand describes
the soldiers' long journey from the United States to Europe and their
efforts to become accustomed to a foreign land.

France
May 19, 1918

Dear Mr. Hiestand.

. . . Very little outside of the general experiences of all who make
the trip has happened since I left home last Christmas Day. The
uncertainty and wonder were over when we mounted the old Ger-

*Soldiers of the American Expeditionary Force arrive at Brest, France,
aboard the steamship* Leviathan, *formerly the Hamburg-American liner*
Vaterland, *May 30, 1918. Committee on Public Information photo.*

WHi(X3)47085

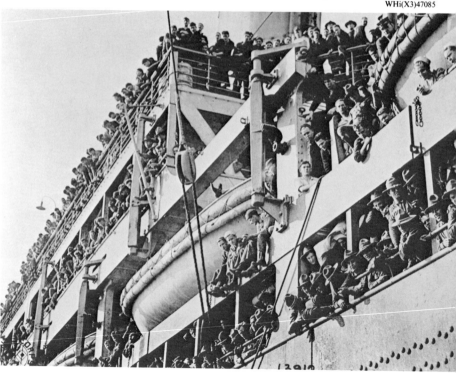

man sea horse[4] just after New Year's but anxiety became a little
more intense. Cold as New York was, the Gulf Stream soon told us
we were gone then when a few days later double watch was put in
the fore top and main top Crow's-nests we felt we were going somewhere. The next day I found myself holding my quaking knees and
shortened breathe 110 feet or more from deck after the stiffest, "rol-
lingest" and highest climb up the rattlers into the foretop watch
basket. The next day we were allowed two meals, both in the day
time, no lights after dark and invited to crawl into our bunks with
life belts on over all our clothes. From that day until we saw the
destroyers like a fine bunch of hunting dogs cutting across our path
fore and aft shedding a smoke screen as they bounced, reeled and
turned to cutting waves again, things were somewhat scary for all
but more for those not on duty than we, the Army, now Navy officers of the watch.

But land came, France at last after almost three weeks on board.
The ground felt good, but then and now not a one of us would
hesitate to walk the wave polished decks again if someone would
yell — "It's all over go back as you will!"

But in France as other places a man must eat. Its the same in Any
or every language but the menu looks queer, or as the colored boys
I am now serving with would say, "Sort of Curious," and unfamil-
iar in an unknown language. Six of us all poor illiterates not knowing more than "Oui! ah Oui!" had a great time ordering that first
meal. We finally finished by telling the calm yet smiling waitress to
carry in a meal. Even this had to be done a-la sign language. We ate
and left a meal behind but we learned a lesson too. . . .

As Ever

Conrad M. Fox

Father Walter A. Beaudette (1884–1962) was born near Chippewa Falls.
He attended Sacred Heart College in Prairie du Chien and the Grand
Seminary in Montreal, Canada, and was ordained as a Catholic priest in
1908 for the diocese of Superior. Beaudette served parishes in Bruce, Rice
Lake, and Rhinelander before enlisting as an army chaplain in 1917.
While in France, Beaudette served with the 14th Engineers Regiment and
corresponded regularly with Albert J. O'Melia, a prominent Rhinelander
attorney. After the war, Beaudette was the pastor of St. Ann's Parish in
Somerset and chaplain at St. Mary's Hospital in Rhinelander.

[4] Possibly the *Vaterland*, a Hamburg-American liner impounded in 1914 and used as a
troop transport for the American Expeditionary Force.

France
November 21, 1917

Dear Al —

Letter-writing had become a difficult art for me. We are commanded to refrain from talking military matters and these things are about all I know. American censorship of mails is rigid. An officer's mail could get him into deep trouble if he were indiscreet. The climate is agreable and disagreable. It is not cold, but very damp, and cloudless. It will remain thus all Winter. Our trip over was safely made. The ocean is vast and it is a hard matter for subs to get a convoy even if it discovers the transports. The army here is very busy in spite of frontal inactivities. I am not far from the front. Our quarters are fairly comfortable: the food is good, and we are well treated. The troops are very busy and manifest no home-sickness.

France is very resigned. The people have set most of their pristine frivolity aside. Food is regulated but there is no sign of want. Some luxuries are scarce because of embargoes in imports. There is one thing that the folks back home cannot send in excess to the boys here and that is tobacco and reading matter. They can send boatloads and car-loads and still the demand will persist. I think a greater publicity should be given to the fact that a stamp on a magazine moves it on to the army where 50 soldiers will literally devour same. The boys will read anything from an essay on the 4th dimension to a prayer-book. It makes no difference how old the magazines are, only they must not fall apart.

More next time. Regards to everyone you meet that I know.

Sincerely,
Chaplain W. A. Beaudette

"I am tiring somewhat of this war"

As many veterans will attest, military life is not all training and fighting, but it still meant a substantial change in living standards for Americans and exposure to new experiences. Men and women from Wisconsin filled their letters home with details about living conditions in France.

During the First World War, Americans realized that recreation for soldiers both at home and abroad was an integral part of the total war effort. The Commission on Training Camp Activities, which consisted of civilian service organizations such as the Y.M.C.A., the Knights of Columbus, the Jewish Welfare Board, and the Salvation Army, ensured that soldiers had access to many of the amenities of home. For example, Y.M.C.A. post and field exchanges sold stationery, stamps, personal articles, and other items. The army also provided movies, organized sporting events, and looked after the moral atmosphere of the military camps.

Born in Eagle, in Waukesha County, Aurel Baker (1886 –1962) was graduated from the Illinois Training School for Nurses in 1912 and volunteered three years later to be a Red Cross nurse in a Russian army hospital in Kiev. Baker enlisted in the U.S. Army Nurses Corps in the fall of 1917 and was assigned to American Base Hospital 36 in Vittel, France. During the German spring offensive in 1918, she was stationed at a hospital at Compiègne, France. After the war, Baker returned to Eagle where she worked as a public health nurse and married Harold Pardee. These letters to her family and her friend Laura provide a rare glimpse of the experience of American women who went to France with the American Expeditionary Force.

France
February 24, 1918

Dearest Sister and "Nicest Brother-in-law in the World"

. . . The most exciting event we have had around here lately was General Pershing's[5] visit last week. He came very unexpectedly so there was no demonstration! You would recognize him easily from his pictures, a tall, severe looking personage. Well he made quite a lot of commotion about the place even though he only stayed a few hours. Our social activities increase daily. We nurses have a literary meeting every Sat night. Last Sat was French History night. A lieutenant, who has been wounded at the front lectured to us and we had music by some of the convalescent patients. We had entertainments on both Washington's and Lincoln's birthdays and movies on Sundays, Tuesdays and Fridays so you will understand why you don't get letters more frequently. I never read so little in my life. Have just finished Royce's "Philosophy of Loyalty"[6] which is the only book I've read in France. Have just had a letter from cousin Annie in which she invited me to spend my furlough with her. Would love to do it but don't know whether I can get permission or not. After March 15, I will be due a 7 day furlough but it seems one must have parents in England in order to visit there. Think I shall ask cousin to write me a letter with the salutation "Dear daughter". . . .

Much love from
Aurel

[5] Major General John J. Pershing (1860–1948) was the commander of the American Expeditionary Force in France.
[6] Josiah Royce, *The Philosophy of Loyalty* (New York, 1908), consisted of a set of lectures arguing that the salvation of the individual could be found through loyalty to a cause.

WHi(X3)47092

*Aurel Baker's French identification card. Aurel Baker Pardee Papers,
State Historical Society of Wisconsin.*

France
April 17, 1918

Dear Laura,

. . . The Y.M.C.A. furnishes a daily (or nightly I should say) entertainment. Last night it was boxing and I surely enjoyed it. The enlisted men of the unit have organized 7 ball teams which makes it possible to have a ball game every day in the week and that is exactly what would happen if it didn't rain quite so often. We have a place to play basket ball also but rain also hinders that a bit. However we do go out picking wild flowers and there are oodles of them; anemonies, primroses, violets cowslips and wild plum blossoms. . . .

From Aurel

> Some of the best accounts of military life in France came from the pen of Chaplain Walter Beaudette. In these two letters to Albert J. O'Melia, he offered detailed accounts of the everyday experiences of the American soldier.

France
May 29, 1918

Dear Al —

You asked for an occasional line. I am in a large tent at present which we are using for recreational purposes. I managed to rent an ancient piano yesterday. It is more valuable as an antique than as a musical instrument but some sounds come out of it. We are fairly well supplied with athletic goods which I procured by means of a limited K.C. fund entrusted to me. Both Y. & K.C. stationery we have in abundance just now. The effect of these conveniences on the morale of the men is noticeable.

We have no cinema views but the men have access to a neighboring large port town where they can be amused. Booze cannot be sold to Americans, and in general the rules are faithfully observed. The drinking cafes are open only from 12–2 P.M. and from 6–8 P.M. The red light districts are all marked and to be merely seen on those streets is a court-martial offense. Our provost guards plus the British guards manage to keep over-amorous chaps away from the dives. There are numerous street-sirens who parade, but the bombing of all towns behind the lines has rendered all cities very dark and uninteresting at night. Besides all soldiers must return to camp at 8:15, with the sun still shining. Venereal troubles in our regiment are almost nil, and intoxication cases are almost unheard of.

I am convinced that the same men of our unit would not lead as cleanly lives in civil life as they must needs do here in the army.

We are camped by the sea-coast, a beautiful spot near a large French town. We take almost daily plunges in the briny. The beach is a dandy. No civilians molest us. The government does not issue bathing costumes so we content ourselves with a plunge à la Adam, without even the conventional oak-leaf. The water is desperately cold, however, and we do not remain in the ocean "a day and a night"[7] as St. Paul did. The simple life appeals to us more. . . .

Sincerely yours,
Chaplain W. A. Beaudette

France
August 17, 1918

Dear Al —

. . . There are no canteens or Y.M.C.A.'s in this area. The K.C.'s are the only ones who have gotten here so far. Practically only K.C. stationery is used for miles around here. Last week I distributed 50,000 sheets of writing paper and envelopes, and the demand for more was loud and insistent. The K.C.'s give away chocolate, cigarettes, and stationery and are making a tremendous hit. The Red Cross does the same, but they are not everywhere. The Y.M.C.A. does excellent work but the doughboys are sore at it, to a certain extent, because they retail goods instead of giving them, although their fund was large. Personally I have much esteem for all three organizations. I delivered some stationery to a neighboring bunch of French aviators who said they had had no writing material for over two weeks. Civilians are not returning at once to these villages. The military must police (clean up) the places first, bury cadavers and arrivals, exterminate flies etc. There are still over 200 unburied enemies within a mile of this billet, but as they lie in a copse on a high hill they are left to be buried last.

I am convinced now that we shall Winter here once more — the last time I hope. Next Summer we ought to win and go home.

There is an American aviation in this village, two squadrons in fact. The "hat in the ring" bunch, and the "jack-ass" squadron[8] — so called from a kicking mule painted on the fuselage. Quentin

---

[7] II Corinthians 11:25.
[8] The 94th and 95th Aero Squadrons respectively. The 95th Aero was also known as the "Kicking Mule" Squadron.

Roosevelt[9] belonged to this outfit, I hear. On a trip two days ago I passed Roosevelt's grave. His demolished "jack-ass" is about 700 feet away. The engine is removed from it. The grave is fixed up nicely for a soldier's, with a rail around it. It will have to be dug up afterwards, for it is not in a good place. It is in a field and will bother the farmer who may disturb it.

Tomorrow we move again, the Lord knows whither. Moving now is not pleasant. We are field troops of the engineer corps, are limited in our baggage to what we carry on our backs. Our officers and men must trek over the dusty highways, sometimes 18 kilometres or more in one day. One company of our engineers hiked 27 miles one day with full pack. If it were not for the awful yellow dust caused by endless lines of lorries, carrions, & ambulances, walking would not be bad, as we rest every few kilometres and smoke a pipeful of tobacco. When we finish our hike we resemble a bunch of small town millers. Everybody whistles on the hike, it puts pep into one. Singing is out of question, it would mean eating up half of France plus umpteen varieties of germs. The infantry going into line rides. One cannot walk a long distance in the hot sun then ferret out machine-guns with much of a heart. . . .

I am tiring somewhat of this war. It is almost a year now for me. But I can stand a year more, I guess. I don't object to the food or pay, both are excellent, but I dislike this billeting in old shell torn villages. My last billet had no roof and only two walls standing. It is a nice billet if it doesn't rain. I had Mass in the village church Sunday which is pretty well shot up. Before I got to the gospel the audience had to shift into the large sanctuary as cakes of plaster came tumbling down each time a heavy lorry passed by on the street.

Our present officers' billet is a fairly good place, there are only three shell holes in the roof and four or five holes punched through the walls. We had a hard time securing the billet. When we came we found that the "Jack-ass" squadron officers had marked the door with chalk. As they had not yet taken possession we marked it over "14th Engrs. Headquarters", and left to get our baggage. In the interim the 55th coast artillery officers came along, erased our names out and placed theirs, and left to get their baggage. We returned and replaced our names and established four sentries with fixed bayonets — we have the billets now. The artillerymen have

---

[9] Quentin Roosevelt (1897–1918), the son of former President Theodore Roosevelt, served in the 95th Aero Squadron and was shot down near Château-Thierry on July 14, 1918. His grave became a sort of shrine for American troops in France, who often broke pieces off of Roosevelt's plane and kept them as souvenirs.

warned us not to do that again or they would send us a package in the shape of a 155 millimetre. After enduring Fritz's 15 inch shells in Picardy a mere 155 is small fry.

Excuse lead pencil. Fritz left us many empty bottles, machineguns, ammunition, but no ink. If one asks for ink from another, one meets with that twinkle in the eye that one would experience if he went to Lewis' hardware and asked to be shown a British tank among the hardware on the shelf.

About two weeks ago we billeted the enlisted men in a large jail along with 62 Fritz prisoners captured by the Yanks. The officers of the regiment moved into a former insane asylum. Our colonel was wired by corps headquarters if all was alright. He wired: "Enlisted men all in jail, and all officers in insane asylum, all well."

Well-wishingly yours,
W. A. Beaudette

Charles Frederic Sammond (1895–1962) was born in Milwaukee and attended Galahad Academy in Hudson. He enlisted in the Wisconsin National Guard in 1913. During the war, Sammond served as a captain with the 32nd Division in France. After the war, he studied law and worked as an attorney in Milwaukee.

France
October 20, 1918

Dear Folks:

... Just censored some mail and the following story was quoted in 90% of them, showing it's popularity. A rumor spread like wildfire that three American women had arrived in a YMCA in a town near here. According to the Stars & Stripes[10] there are lots of such women, but we have been so darned far in front, that we haven't seen a French woman for over a month, and an American for three. As a matter of fact, I haven't spoken to an American woman in 7 months. However, referring to above rumor all the boys not on duty rushed over and fell in line for the hot chocolate in preparation. The line grew long, and the ladies needed some water carried. One of them stepped to the line and asked one of the men "What Division"? "32nd".[11] She asked others. Same answer. Then she called out "Are there any men not in the 32nd"? Three men spoke

[10] A military newspaper.

[11] The 32nd Division, comprised mostly of men from Wisconsin and Michigan, spent six months under fire from May to November, 1918, with only ten days in a rest area. This unit suffered 14,000 casualties while playing a crucial role in the Aisne-Marne, Oise-Aisne, and Meuse-Argonne offensives. Known as the "Red Arrow" division, the men of the 32nd were the first American soldiers to set foot on German soil.

up and said they were in the — th Div (A "National Army" Division of only two or three months front experience.) The lady then said "Will you please get these pails filled down at the spring. I don't like to ask the 32nd to do it. They have been fighting so long and so hard." Needless to say, the ladies are very popular with the 32nd and not so popular with the — th.

Censoring Mail is always a rather melancholy job. The men are now accustomed to censors, and write perfectly freely, and it is like boldly listening to one end of a telephone conversation, over and over again. On top of it, it is raining and one of the men is playing a violin in the next room. Another is singing in accompaniment. These choices suit the weather. All about "Goodbye" and "Farewell" and interupted love in general. Somebody sent up a book of war songs and we have been deriding them and otherwise enjoying them. What ferocious fighters those songwriters be. They inform the world at large that "we'll knock the 'hell' out of Wilhelm". Also

Y.M.C.A. workers dispense food from a rolling canteen to front-line troops of the 32nd Division in Alsace, Germany, June 22, 1918. Signal Corps photo.
WHi(X3)47086

"we'll make the Kaiser do the Goose step to a good American rag". Also "Democracies Calling" in tune with "Autocracies falling". Incidently the pines are whispering Dixieland in Alsace.

Al asks me to send him a German Helmet. I'll try to do so at first opportunity. It's easy enough to get one but it's hard to mail it. I never sent one before, because I felt kind of false pretenses. You picture a helmet as having been wrested from some snarling struggling Boch. As a matter of fact, we get the helmets off dead ones, or out of old huts, and all we ever see of live Boches is through a telescope and thats all he sees of us. When we do see each other thru a glass, we promptly try to kill each other with "H.E." (High explosive) but never know if we do, except what prisoners tell us. . . .

Yours
Fritz

Lyle G. Phillips was born in Waupun in 1894 but grew up in nearby Fond du Lac. From 1912 to 1917 he worked for the *Fond du Lac Reporter* as a reporter and editor. During the war, Phillips served with the 7th Infantry Division in France. After the war, he returned to the United States to attend the University of Wisconsin (B.S., 1922) and Rush Medical College in Chicago (M.D., 1924). Phillips eventually moved to Honolulu, Hawaii, where he practiced medicine until his death in 1980.

France
November 4, 1918

Dear Mother:

Today is election day back in the States, & I don't know the name of a single candidate. That is a funny condition of affairs, isn't it? Particularly since I always have been so interested & mixed up in elections. Tonight is the first election night in years that hasn't meant more work for me. . . .

Here no one cares much about politics though. Roosevelts & Tafts[12] answer to President Wilson caused a unanimous laugh at our mess the other night, but that was all. Wilson surely is popular here with everybody. . . .

Your loving son
Lyle

[12] Phillips may be referring to the joint statement issued by Theodore Roosevelt and William Howard Taft in which they denounced President Wilson's patriotic appeal to vote Democratic. In a joint statement released on November 1, 1918, by the Republican National Committee, the former presidents asked "all Americans who are Americans first" to vote Republicans into Congress.

Carl N. Jacobs was born in Stevens Point in 1895, and after graduating from high school he began working in his father's small insurance firm. In 1918, Jacobs enlisted in the U.S. Army and rose to the rank of sergeant with the Ordnance Corps of the American Expeditionary Force in France. After his discharge in 1919, Jacobs returned to Stevens Point and to his growing insurance business. He became president of Sentry Insurance in 1930 and chairman of the board in 1960. Jacobs also served as treasurer and vice-president of the U.S. Chamber of Commerce and remained a prominent community leader until his death in 1980.

France
November 8, 1918

Dear Dad:
. . . It seems that everyone in writing me seems to kid me about cooties.[13] Well now take it from me they are nothing to kid about. After you have scratched all day and then each night peeled off your undershirt and hunted for "big game" and then scratched all night there is no fun in it. Have had them twice but have gotten rid of them by taking a good hot bath and then throwing away my underclothes. One of the fellows said he fooled them by turning his inside out every day and it took them just a day to get back to the inside again. Another one of our fellows heard that a hot iron would get rid of them so he heated his mess kit on the fire and it sure was a sight to see him at work. At times there are scenes which make a person forget the seriousness of this business but it only takes one of Jerry's shells or a look around the country to bring it all back. . . .

With Love,
Carl

Kenneth S. White (1897–1976) attended River Falls Teachers College and the University of Wisconsin Law School. In 1917 he joined the army and served overseas with the 6th Heavy Artillery of the American Expeditionary Force. White returned to law school after the war and eventually became a partner in his father's River Falls law firm. Involved in state Republican party politics, White served as a state senator, district attorney for Pierce County, and circuit court judge. During the Second World War, he commanded a battalion in the Wisconsin National Guard.

France
November 10, 1918

Dear Mother, —
. . . Our company has adopted a couple of Belgian orphans thru the Red Cross and last pay day we each contributed 5% of our pay

---

[13] "Cooties" (body lice) were a major annoyance for front-line troops unable to bathe regularly. Often the first stop for soldiers on leave was the delousing station in the rear areas.

to support them during the coming year. A number of American units are adopting Belgian and French children and not to be outdone we decided that the 6th Heavy ought to follow suit. When we came to vote on whether we wanted a boy or a girl the company split, so we compromised by adopting both. We contribute $100 and the Red Cross takes care of them for us for a year. That's a very cheap way to raise a family, isn't it? . . .

With Love,
Kenneth

"So you see it is all a game of chance"

"In war it is comforting to be a fatalist," Glenn Garlock wrote in 1927. "If there is a bomb or bullet bearing your number no dodging will escape it." American soldiers like Garlock found little that was encouraging about modern warfare once they witnessed the destruction three years of fighting had caused the French countryside. Heavy artillery, poison gas, barbed wire, and machine guns combined to make the World War I battlefield a miserable and desolate place. Soldiers dehumanized the German enemy with nicknames such as "Hun," "Fritz," or the "Boche." After the advent of trench warfare, success was measured in yards and "acceptable" casualty rates sometimes turned costly advances into "victories." In late 1917, French soldiers reached their breaking point and mutinied against their own officers. American doughboys fortunately were never exposed to the horrors of trench warfare for as long as the French. As the four letters presented below suggest, however, even a brief glimpse of no-man's-land made an indelible impression on the minds of many young American soldiers.

Private Eldon J. Canright was graduated from Wauwatosa High School in 1912. After working in a Milwaukee wholesale grocery, Canright moved to Chicago to become a salesman for a manufacturing firm. In May, 1917, he enlisted in an Illinois National Guard Unit and was later transferred to the 149th Field Artillery of the 42nd Division of the American Expeditionary Force in France. Canright's letters provide rich description of life on the front for a member of Pershing's famous "Rainbow Division."

France
March 14, 1918

My dear Mrs. Pierson:

I am going to try and describe to you what it is like in the trenches. Understand, of course, I cannot describe any certain battle, but what I am going to describe can and does take place anywhere along our front.

Soldiers of the 32nd Division on duty in the trenches. Signal Corps photo.

Try and imagine yourself standing in one of the trenches on the "fire control" step, or in one of the advanced "listening posts." It is a beautiful evening, with the stars shining overhead and everything is so calm and peaceful that it is hard to realize that there are hundreds, nay thousands, of guns and tens of thousands of soldiers lying waiting and watching. Perhaps you have been on duty for some time and you are tired and as everything is quiet you look at your watch and it is between two and three o'clock in the morning. Your thoughts turn toward home, and you wonder what your friends are doing as it is early evening there. You wonder if they can see the same stars that you can see overhead. Then all of a sudden a rocket goes up, bursting over "No Man's Land," casting a red or perhaps a green light. That is the signal and then "Hell breaks loose." (That describes it so pardon the word.) Guns begin to roar and pound on all sides of you — the noise is deafening. You can see the flashes of the guns as they fire and you can hear the "whine" of the shells as they go through the air. In fact, you can tell when a shell is coming toward you as you can hear it "whining" as it comes toward you and all you can do is to crouch down and pray God it will not strike where you are. If it does it will be "taps" for you (as we say), or rather what is left of you! You can tell a "high explosive" shell from a "gas shell" because when a high explosive shell bursts it gives a sharp "crash," destroying everything near it, while a "gas shell" explodes with a "pop," very similar to a sound a bottle makes when breaking, as a gas shell is filled with a liquid (i.e. — gas condensed under high pressure, which instantly vaporizes on bursting). Of course, if a gas shell bursts near you, you must stop breathing instantly, until you have put on and adjusted your gas-mask! Then you may have to work for hours with that on. I could write whole pages about the various gases used in this war and their different effects on the human body, but just let me say that they are all horrible and cause a lingering and painful death. I pray God that if I have to give up my life in this war it will be with a bullet and not gas! At intervals between the roaring of the big guns you can hear the "spit" of the rifles as the infantry open fire and high over head you will hear the purring of the airplanes as they go up to make observations, range corrections, etc. And the enemy airplanes go up to give battle and you can hear the "drumming" of their machine guns as they fight, too. At about five minute intervals star shells are sent up. They burst away up over "No Man's Land," and hang suspended in the air, casting a very bright light over "No Man's Land." And in the town behind our lines you will see the powerful searchlights sweeping the sky for any enemy airplane that might slip through our lines. If one does, their anti-aircraft guns open up, too, and then more airplanes come up. And so it goes.

A day battle is just the same, only our hardest fighting is at night. And what makes me sick is to see the wounded horses and mules; they do not understand it all and are perfectly innocent anyway. So you see it is all a game of chance; if no shell strikes near you, or no stray bullet finds you, you are lucky, that's all.

. . . I know nearly every little French kid in town. The little boys love to put on my steel helmet and belt, etc., and play soldier, boylike. When they have a gun on their hip they think they are "it." But I wish you could see them stand at "attention" and salute. Believe me, these little children know what war means!

Sincerely,
E. J. Canright

France
May 2, 1918

My Dear Jane:

. . . I am stationed with one of the most advanced batteries. We live, of course, in an abri[14] many feet below the ground. The abri is lined with steel and heavy beams and is covered with many feet of rocks and earth. It is always cold and very damp. The floor is covered with slimy mud and water, even though we try to bale it out every day. And, of course, our quarters are very cramped as we sleep in tiers, one above the other. You cannot sit up straight in bed. If you try to you will bump your head against the bed above you. And it is very dark as, of course, there are no windows and only one small door, and that does not let in much light as it leads down from the trench above. However, we have been so busy giving the Hun hell (pardon me), that we have very little chance to sleep, and when we do we are so tired that we just pull off our boots and crawl into bed and go right off to sleep, even though the big guns all around us are pounding away so that the air is constantly filled with their "shrieks" and "whines" and even way down where we are, one can feel the earth tremble from the shock of the guns as they fire. Of course, I am here to take care of anyone that gets hurt, and that is all I am supposed to do, but nevertheless I take turns "standing at the guns" and hauling ammunition, etc., and that is no easy task when you consider that we have to walk along a long, narrow

---

[14] A dugout or cavity in a trench that soldiers used for shelter from artillery.

trench, running from the abri to the gun pits. The trench always has six inches to a foot of water in the bottom, and on the bottom there may be some slippery, slimy boards or rocks, and the sides of the trench are just wet clay and mud. And then, to add to your difficulties, it is roofed over, which makes it dark as a pocket, and in places it is not deep enough to allow you to walk standing straight up, so unless you are pretty well acquainted with the position you are apt to get some awful cracks on your "dome," but thanks to your steel helmet it won't knock you out. You'll just "see stars" for a few minutes. One has to be pretty careful when carrying ammunition through there. It kind of gives you a creepy feeling when you think what might happen if you should slip when carrying a big shell in your arms and it should strike on a rock just right! You would be "pushing daisies up in skeleton park, tout de suite." . . .

Love,
E. J. Canright

Lee Francis Pickett was born in the Marathon County community of Spencer during the winter of 1894. He was graduated from Rice Lake High School in 1911, and four years later he enrolled in a two-year teaching program at the Oshkosh Normal School. Pickett joined the army in November 1917, and after two months of training at Fort Sheridan he arrived in France as a second lieutenant in the 102nd Infantry Regiment of the 26th Division. Twice cited for bravery in battle, Pickett was mortally wounded in the summer of 1918 during the Allied counterattack at Château Thierry and died in October of 1918. Pickett's letters to his mother reveal the reactions of a small-town Wisconsin boy encountering what was then the most destructive war in human history.

France
April 25, 1918

My dear mother:

. . . Many song birds, chiefly sky larks, make the mornings beautiful with their songs. Even on the front line while the whistling shells and bursting high explosives make everything hideous, these little birds keep on with their cheerful little songs. Sometimes I wonder why it is that animals calling themselves civilized human beings dare to call themselves such and carry on such a war, while the little birds whom we class among the lower type of animals can spread so much cheer and gladness about on this earth. . . .

Love and best wishes to all, and the big share to you.

Yours —
Lee F. Pickett

Although Glenn Garlock sat in training camp throughout the Spanish-American War (see pp. 5–9), he saw his fair share of action as a lieutenant colonel by the time the First World War was over. "War is a wasteful and destructive enterprise," Garlock reminisced in 1927. "In those days no sacrifice was too great, and nothing that impeded progress too valuable to be wrecked." In his letters to his wife, Anna, Garlock eloquently described some of the hard decisions he had to make as an officer.

France
June 1, 1918

Dear Wife: —

. . . I have some duties up here that almost hurt. There are roads and paths where men must move to reach their place and I must issue the orders. In the wink of an eye the Boche could cover these roads with shells and he does. If he ever caught a group it would

WHi(X3)47124

Glenn W. Garlock, c. 1918.
Courtesy Mildred Garlock Morris.

mean some losses and I worry some until I know the danger spots are passed.

Another duty comes that I dont like. It is the sending of patrols out in front nights. We have had several out and no body lost but tonight it might be changed and a patrol meet with a mishap. So it goes. Duties that must be done and someone must issue the orders, give the mission, make the plan. I remember someone saying "you cannot make an omelet without breaking some eggs." It sounds harsh when applied to men but we all take our chances, probably our Doctor takes the most of any for his 1st Aid Station is shelled every day almost.

I think none of us like shelling but at night we set at the table under the trees and laugh and joke over the days experience. One night the "Medico" said "I will sure kick the whey out of the next fellow that asks me to chip in on a 4th of July celebration." I dont know but what I would too. I have heard more shells explode and more big guns fire than I have heard all my life before. Maybe I have said it before but I am certain it is true that more shells have landed in the sector my battalion holds in the last 10 days than were fired at the whole U.S. Army in the Spanish American War. . . .

It is time to go to bed so I will finish this page and retire. I will make a few confessions. For over 20 years I have trained, studied, worked to be worth something as a military man. Some of the best days of my life and some of my hardest efforts have been spent at the game. I have wished to try myself out. The try out has come and I do not find it so wonderful after all. I am not a coward nor have I been unsuccessful in leading men but after all I can think of nothing quite so satisfactory as being home at ease and at peace with you and the children about. How I would love to romp with the youngsters for an evening and have you all with me and yet after all until the last shot is fired or at least until I am unfit for service my heart will always be with those who hold the lines. I would not be satisfied with the easy path of civil life while I could be of use here. When the thing is over they can send me home in a row boat if necessary and I'll say that I have seen enough of the world to last a lifetime. Always down in my heart my love goes out to you and to ours.

Glenn W. Garlock

WHi(X3)19277

"When the thing is over they can send me home in a row boat if necessary and I'll say that I have seen enough of the world to last a lifetime."
American troops outside a dugout, Alsace, Germany, June 20, 1918.

"Aeroplanes are the winners"

"It looked as though the war would keep up indefinitely," Billy Mitchell remembered in 1926, "until either the airplanes brought an end to the war or the contending nations dropped from sheer exhaustion." Although they first appeared as reconnaissance forces, airplanes developed more lethal capabilities such as aerial bombing, the strafing of enemy troops, and "dogfighting" among themselves. The United States sent its airplanes to Europe with the Army Signal Corps, then formed a separate Air Service of the National Army in May 1918. In World War I, American pilots reported 776 enemy planes and seventy-two observation balloons destroyed while losing only 290 planes. Flying was also dangerous work for Americans, as the Army Air Service suffered 569 battle casualties, 319 accident deaths, and 335 deaths from other causes. Despite these high losses, American planes performed a vital role in ending the far bloodier ground war in Europe. In the letters below, Father Walter Beaudette, Eldon Canright, and Lyle Phillips expressed the amazement of American soldiers who witnessed this revolutionary innovation in warfare.

WHi(X3)47083

Although the planes appear quaint by today's standards, air power represented cutting-edge technology during the First World War. Committee on Public Information photo.

France
February 21, 1918

Dear Al —
. . . Aeroplanes are the winners, send them at once. This year will be plane year. If we have enough planes the war is won. We get bombed very often now. By *we* I mean our camp area. Not that the enemy selects our camp particularly but he spots it along with other objectives. We were bombed four times a while ago in one night. Last night we had two visits but no bombs fell directly in the camp. Planes do not come singly but in fleets at least 3 or 4, but once here must have been 15 or 20. The racket all around was fierce. Archies[15] and Machine guns were firing at Fritz and he savagely barked back wherever he would see the flames of the guns. We stood outside watching the show until the machines would arrive overhead — then presto, we scattered to our holes in the ground, sunk our heads in our shoulders and wondered "where, oh! where, will the next one fall." These bombing stunts of the Germans are a source of funmaking around the stove-pipes,[16] but *after* the raid is over only. During the awful din you never saw a more solemn faced out-fit than the 14th Engineers of the Regular Army. If I were not for the appalling racket made by the bombs I do not think one would mind them much for we know that they cannot be dropped accurately at all. . . .

W. A. Beaudette

France
July 8, 1918

My dear Folks:
. . . During the daytime there are a great many airplanes flying overhead, constantly trying to "see" what the other side is doing. We have witnessed some very exciting air battles. It is nothing unusual to see anywhere from two to two dozen airplanes fighting and chasing each other in and out of the clouds as they maneuver to get into position to fire — we can hear the "spitting" of their machine guns as they fire; sometimes you can hear them fighting when they are above the clouds, too! And twice a very daring German aviator flew down over our position and turned his machine gun on us! We could hear the "whang and spit" of the bullets as they struck the

---

[15] Anti-aircraft guns.
[16] As Beaudette explained in his letter of March 12, 1918 (printed below), "stove-pipe" was a slang term for rumors and stories exchanged by American soldiers because they originated around the exhaust pipes of stoves in the huts.

ground within a few feet of us! He flew so low that we could see the black cross on the plane and see the aviators shooting at us! But they didn't stay long. They would just shoot down and fire and then away they'd go before we had a chance to shoot back at them. . . .

Love,

E. J. Canright

France
October 21, 1918
Dear Mother: —
. . . Tonight is a wonderful moonlight night and the planes of both sides are active. A squadron of 25 American planes passed over, Germany-bound, this afternoon & hasn't returned yet. The sky is striped with search-light beams & every few minutes the anti-aircraft guns' shells go "pop-pop-pop" as they make life miserable for some boche way up above. We can see a little flash up in the sky, then the growing puff of smoke as the moonlight strikes it, and finally, a few seconds later, we hear the sound of the explosion. . . .

Your son
Lyle [Phillips]

"It is almost more than you can stand"

The incredible loss of life and human suffering caused by modern warfare were well known by the time of the American arrival in France. The British suffered 57,470 casualties (more than 19,000 killed) in a single day at the Battle of the Somme in 1916. That same year at Verdun, more than a million French and German soldiers were killed or wounded during the course of a single battle. By comparison, the United States suffered 50,385 battle deaths, 51,447 killed as a result of disease, and 204,002 wounded during the war. In the seven letters printed below, Wisconsin men and women tried to put into words the shock, fear, and sadness that accompanied the death and destruction of the First World War.

Even though Billy Mitchell was already familiar with the horrors of battle as a young lieutenant in the Philippines (see pp. 20–24), he was deeply moved by a personal tragedy in France. Mitchell had learned to fly an airplane in 1916, and a year later he was in France with the American army. In August, 1917, Mitchell got his chance to prove the merits of air power when he was appointed Commander of the Air Service of the American Expeditionary Force. His meteoric rise was tempered by the death of his brother John in an airplane crash in May, 1918. In this letter to his mother, Mitchell described the grief felt by many soldiers who lost friends and family during the war.

WHi(X28)4240
General William "Billy" Mitchell, c. 1925.

France
June 26, 1918

My dear dear Mummy

. . . John's loss I suppose was the hardest thing that ever happened to me. To begin with he was my only brother, he was so much younger that he was like a son, and in addition he was the same as a great friend. He had every quality that I wanted in a brother and admired in a man. I suppose he was very nearly the dearest living thing in the world to me. There is little use talking about it because it is all over. I always thought that I would go first and as neither of us had any sons we decided to have one of Janet's[17] sons take our name in case we both went. I have not seen Mitchell about this, but I want it done in the event that I go because otherwise there will be no descendents of our direct line named Mitchell. I think about

[17] Sister of Billy Mitchell and wife of Mitchell Mackie.

you, I suppose, every hour of every day, and I know what it means to you to have John gone, and just how calmly you are taking it outwardly and how deeply you feel inwardly. You can be sure of one thing. No mother could be prouder of a son than you can be of John. His grave is about four Kilometers north of Toul, in the Sevastopol hospital cemetery. He lies among many comrades and friends. I have employed a farmer to keep growing flowers on it always and his squadron the 1st. Aero, put a large everlasting wreath with purple flowers and green leaves which is beautiful. I am in excellent health, and command all our air troops on the line. No body ever had better troops under him or a better command. . . .

Your affectionate Son

Wm. Mitchell

Victor Morris was born in 1889 in Milwaukee. He was graduated from Harvard University in 1912 and returned to his home state to study engineering at the University of Wisconsin. During the war, Morris served in the Engineering Corps and rose to the rank of major by the time he returned to the United States in 1919. During the 1920s, Morris managed the Foster Morris Construction Company in Milwaukee, and during World War II he established the Safety Engineering Company. He remained as head of the latter firm until his death in 1964.

France

November 8, 1918

Dear father —

. . . During an advance the killed in action are buried very quickly — & all over the battlefields are small grave yards — ten or fifteen rough wooden crosses with these small aluminum identification tags tied to them — sometimes a helmet on the cross, or a rifle with bayonet stuck in at the foot of the grave. Not very beautiful grave yards — but nothing physical in this war is beautiful. I read that they talk about bringing our dead back to the states.[18] I hope they dont — their graves here are honorable — & if they were brought back it would mean that a great many mothers & relatives would be horror stricken — both at the necessarily primitive ways of burial on the battle field — & at what "killed in action" may mean. It's best for the people to think of "killed in action" as being killed by a bullet wound through the heart in an attack — they need not know

[18] Although many families asked the War Department to send home the bodies of their fallen relatives, most Americans chose to leave the graves in France. In 1930 the War Department offered 30,000 "Gold Star Mothers" an all-expenses-paid trip to visit their sons' graves in Europe. Six thousand mothers accepted.

what utter destruction it sometimes means. If I should get mine I certainly hope you'll want me left over here. . . .

Affectionately
Vic

As one of the more than 10,000 nurses with the American Expeditionary Force, Margaret Rowland was an eyewitness to the horrible consequences of modern warfare. Soldiers wounded by artillery, machine guns, and bayonets almost filled the 153 American military hospitals to their capacity of 48,000 beds by late 1918. In addition to being exposed to physical injury and death, soldiers on both sides heard and shared macabre stories of dismemberment and other atrocities. These two letters from Rowland to her family provide a graphic account of the horrors of modern warfare.

Mesgrigny, France
c. July 10, 1918

Dearest old Popsie and bunch —

. . . At one and the same time there was a croix de guerre[19] decoration, a battle in the air — German and French planes, an American boy being buried, and one dying in the ward. It was horrible! Oh, when you are right face to face with the very biggest things in the world, death and human suffering, you realize how small you are — and how dependent you are upon God and his Will. You do not realize how you struggle thru the heart wrenching things you do when you think of it afterward. You just cannot let yourself dwell on that part of it. You have to look thru this telescope lined with scenes tragic and sorrowful and see the glowing light of the purpose and the outcome of it all at the end, but it is awfully hard not to focus your telescope on some of these sad scenes, such as our poor boys crying for their mothers and entreating you not to let them die so far from home! "Oh, just see if you can't get me home!" Oh, how they love the U.S.A. It is almost more than you can stand sometimes. . . .

Oh, and speaking of colonial troops. You know of course that the Senagalese troops are negroes from the French colonies in Africa.[20] They are fierce looking things and the Boche are scared to death of them and you really cannot blame them when you hear this story!

[19] A military decoration established by the French government in 1915.
[20] More than 200,000 Senegalese and other West African troops fought for France during the war. They quickly acquired a reputation for savagery, partly because of their effectiveness in personal combat but mostly from existing racial stereotypes of "barbaric" Africans.

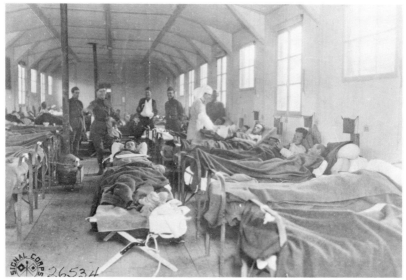

WHi(X3)47077

Lieutenant Harry Humphreys entertains wounded troops at American Evacuation Hospital #114, Fleury-sur-Aire, France, October 8, 1918. Signal Corps photo.

A fierce looking fellow came into a hospital badly wounded, but in one hand he tightly clutched his kit bag very bulgy and queer looking — nothing could make him drop this and it was only when he was under ether that they were able to unloosen his grasp. What was their horror when they opened it to find a fat, healthy German's head. I wish it has been the Kaiser's. Rather an unpleasant souvenir on a warm day. Others have been seen wearing long strings of German's ears around their necks. They fight with fierce looking knives and just live in No Man's Land at night. . . .

All my love.

Muggs

France
August 28, 1918

Dearest Pops & family:

. . . I struggled out of bed, climbed into my clothes, flew over to the operating room, arriving there at 9:30, and there I stayed until 7:30 the next morning. We did operation after operation — and dressings in between. We dug great hunks of eclat[21] from horrible smelling wounds, some smooth machine gun bullets, and ampu-

[21] Splinters or fragments from artillery shells.

tated a few fingers. I saw one amputation of both legs, above the knee. It was awful! The poor devil. We were so tired that day that we just fell into bed and slept until noon. . . .

Yesterday afternoon I went to Troyes and bought some cigarettes for the Red Cross to give the patients. I got back at six o'clock P.M. and discovered that I was guard for the whole hospital for the whole night. It was ghastly! One man who was gassed was breathing his last — and I had to go around after sitting by him and hearing him laboring for breath (his lungs are completely destroyed) and make rounds thru the other dark wards. It was ghostly and spooky. The man died early this morning, poor thing.

Until next time, Farewell.

Muggs

Lee Pickett was one of many Americans wounded in action. He recovered from the leg wound he described in this letter only to be killed during the final two weeks of the war.

France
August 1, 1918

My dear mother:

. . . We reached the first objective of our attack without much trouble. It was while trying to close a slight gap between us the the unit on the left that I stepped into the way of a machine gun bullet. It didn't hurt much but bothered me when I crawled back toward our lines. After wrapping a bandage around the hole which was bleeding worst, I started back toward the village, using a German rifle for a crutch. By resting every little ways I managed to get along quiet well, but a couple of Red Cross boys carried me the last part of the trip into the village. There a doctor bandaged the wound and an hour or so later I started for a Ford ambulance ride, our first stop was at a Field Ambulance Station. There I got an injection of the anti-tetanus serum. From there I was moved through two field hospitals, and an evacuation hospital to an American hospital train. And that was some train. We traveled nearly twenty-four hours, altho that doesn't mean that we averaged forty miles an hour by any means. It was about noon on the twenty-second when we reached this place. The worst cases were taken care of first, of course, and so some of us were just looked at that day. . . .

Yours,
Lee F. Pickett

In addition to being subject to physical danger, soldiers sometimes broke under the strain of constant enemy shelling. In this letter to his wife, Glenn Garlock described both the physical and psychological wounds suffered by Americans during the war.

France
August 27, 1918
Dear Anna: —
   . . . Today I stood for a few moments in a dressing station while a few of our men were being given 1st aid. Here was a young corporal with a bullet through the foot just below his ankle, another with a cut up leg, another with a hole in his arm, one gassed, one with a bloody head, here a slender boyish Boche. None murmured or complained, each was bandaged, had a shot of anti-toxin injected under

WHi(X3)27256
The first stop for the wounded was often a field hospital near the front lines. Here Allied troops receive treatment in a ruined church in Neuville, France, September 20, 1918. Signal Corps photo.

the skin of his abdomen, maybe some morphine too, and was carried out or helped to the waiting ambulances to go back bumpy miles to the field hospitals for the operation and then blighty.[22] Sometimes when the fight is hard and the poor devils must lie in the rain, no food for hours even days, bullets, shells and gas threatening day and night I fancy a slight wound must be a welcome relief. Men sometimes go crazy from the devilish strain of being under shellfire. It is not so much the real danger as the thought of the danger that comes from the shriek and bang of the shells. If one can have work to keep his mind off the noise it helps a whole lot. For 16 hours in my little battle there were shells coming over all the time besides three gas attacks and yet the longer it lasted the more contempt I had for the pesky things. Early in the game one came very close to me and my runner, say a rod away, and went off with a devil of a noise and left us both whole and since then I haven't been so scared. It was a small one however. I would hate to be near when a big fellow busted but I have known of some mighty lucky escapes from these too. . . .

Glenn W. Garlock

Wartime losses were not limited to combatants. Like many other soldiers, Private Eldon Canright was deeply moved by the suffering of the French civilian population.

France
November 8, 1918

My dear Folks:
You have no doubt seen pictures of some of the battlefields over here, but you cannot fully realize the horror and the desolation and waste of the country that has been fought over, unless you have *actually* been there and seen the fields torn with shell holes and the roads and bridges mined and destroyed and the torn and twisted stumps of the trees standing like sentinels guarding the dead! And here and there you see the remains of what was *once* a town, but now is nothing but a pile of broken bricks and burned timbers! And everywhere you see — and sometimes *smell* — the bodies of the dead lying in every conceivable position, among the refuse and broken equipment that always litters a battlefield. That is the kind of country I have been living in for *weeks*! . . .
At night we could see the towns in front of us burning — the bright glare illuminating the sky and farther back would be just the

[22] British slang for going home.

dull, red glow on the horizon. It was a thrilling sight but it made one eager to go on and punish the fiends who were doing it! However, the last two or three days we have made things so hot for "Fritz" that he hasn't had a chance to carry off all the civilians and burn the towns — he has just retreated taking with him all the male civilians who were able to do any work and leaving the old and the feeble behind! It is pathetic to see them. They put white flags on the church tower and in the windows of their homes so we wouldn't shell the town — or what was left of it! Sometimes the Germans took advantage of this and would place machine guns in the houses and fire at us knowing that we wouldn't shell *them* because of the civilians; but in that case we would flank the town on either side, and then Old Fritz had to get out or be taken prisoner! But he had no consideration for the civilians as he has a nice trick of placing bombs and mines with time fuses in the buildings and houses, and timing them so they will explode after we get there. So we always have to look for them when we take a town; but some of them are so cleverly concealed that we cannot find them and every little while there will be a terrific explosion and bricks and tile and mortar go flying in the air and what was a house a few minutes before is now just a pile of broken stone! But that isn't enough damage to satisfy Fritz so when he thinks we are in the town he begins shelling it. Of course we soldiers are used to that and don't mind it, but it makes one sick to see the poor frightened civilians running for shelter and seeing their homes hit with shells, tearing great holes in the roofs and walls!

I could write pages of the stories that the civilians told me of their sufferings — how they were made to work twelve hours a day in the fields, and hauling and making war supplies, etc. — even the children and the young girls, and how the Germans took the good flour that the French government sent the civilians away from them and gave them their dirty, rotten pumpernickle — and little enough of that! And they were not allowed to visit from town to town or even write or receive any letters! And when the Germans left they took everything they could carry — even the rings and watches and the gold or silver crucifixes that the poor people had. They left them practically nothing. Can you imagine living like that for years? . . .

Love,

E. J. Canright

"War is a great teacher and I have learned many lessons"

Wartime correspondence offered American soldiers an opportunity to
reflect on the war, its impact, and its meaning. Chaplain Walter Beaudette
speculated on the impact of the war on the French landscape and about
the end of the war. Eldon Canright offered his meditations on the irony of
giving first aid to wounded German aviators and on his reasons for
fighting. Victor Morris confessed his mixed feelings about not being in
combat, while Glenn Garlock was awestruck by the size and diversity of
the Allied war effort. Together these letters provide a sample of the
reflections of Wisconsin soldiers on their participation in what would be
the most memorable event of their lives.

France
March 12, 1918

Dear Al —

I'll air a view or two of mine about the war and we'll see how
close we guess together. Such guesses here are called "stove-pipes,"
because they originate near the four-inch pipes of our huts. But I
really have far more confidence in a soldier's "stove-pipes" than in
the pronunciciamentos made by chaps in the States who write articles. As an instance I would point to the article appearing in a late
Scientific American where the question is debated whether the shell-
torn fields of France will be arable and productive after the war.
Doubt is expressed whether the fields will yield. Now all that sounds
very absurd to a muddy Yank at the front. Only in certain areas,
limited in size, are the shell-holes very numerous. The shell-holes of
France will not average one shell hole per 20 acres. Regarding duds
the plows and harrows will not set them off because they failed to
explode when they hit the ground with fearful impact.

Anyhow thousands of Chinamen are salvaging behind the lines
and get so much per dud found. Duds will be as scarce as Kaisers
after the war.

We have many "stove-pipes" about the impending Fritz drive. It
is now overdue. The British Tommies,[23] with whom we are working, carry a chip on the shoulder and defy Fritz to do his dog-
gonest. This last word reminds me of a story I heard. Some cow-
boys placed a cross over the grave of a deceased cow-puncher with
the words: "Here lies Slim Harris; he did his damndest, the angels
couldn't do no damnder."

The many British I meet, and also every one of us Americans are
very optimistic about the final out-come. Our only apprehension is

---

[23] "Tommy" was the nickname for a British soldier.

lest the war may not end this year 1918. We do not like the Winter months. It is quite probable, we think, that the Germans will cry "hold enough" in 1918. But again there remains the probability that the end is brought about only by an overwhelming army of Americans!

I guess we shall know pretty well where we are at after the promised "strafe" of the Kaiser has taken place.[24] This battle will probably last many weeks, even all Summer. I am anxious for it to start and so is everybody around here. The Tommies in the trenches where they are not far apart from the Germans yell out to the Germans every now and then: "Come on with your 'strafe,' Fritz." But it has no affect, apparently. Fritz never even replies, save to say: "You chust vait, Tommy." This is trench "stove-pipe" carried back by the Tommies as they return on our narrow gauge Trains.

In some respects we are better off here than the folks home. We get meat, potatoes, bread, coffee, and sugar every day. We never have pastries because we get no flour. For dessert we smoke and exchange officers' "stove-pipes" which are only 1% more valuable than those of the enlisted men. . . .

Sincerely yours,
W. A. Beaudette

France
August 2, 1918

Cher Ami:

I wrote you a letter yesterday P.M. but have not had a chance to mail it yet. However I am glad of it, because last night we had the good fortune to bring down a Hun airplane. Several of them flew over just before dark and fired at us with their machine guns and we "opened up" on them with our machine guns and the rest of us seized our German rifles and ammunition and also fired at them and believe me it was some noise. But it's great sport and very exciting. Well, you can imagine our joy when we saw one turn around and start to come down! I saw him just skimming over the tree tops and saw where he was going to land, so I started after him on the run. They lit in a field but purposely skimmed along the ground and ran the machine into the woods to damage it so that we couldn't use it — See? Of course, it hit the trees and broke the wings and propeller, altho the engine and body were all right. A Frenchman and I were

---

[24] By 1918, the element of surprise had all but disappeared as the war entered its fourth year. Thus, the German spring offensives of 1918 were anticipated by both sides with dread and impatience.

the first ones to reach them, and the aviators, there were two of them, stepped out of their machine and held up their hands. They started to walk towards us but one of them staggered and fell. I saw that he was wounded so I dropped down to examine his wounds and give him first aid, while the Frenchman kept the other one covered with his rifle, as you can't trust a Hun — he might have shot me altho I was giving first aid to his companion. The pilot was wounded in several places, I discovered, after I had taken off his leather headgear and goggles and leather coat, etc. He was shot in the shoulder and on the leg and then I dug a shrapnel bullet out of his back. You can imagine my surprise when he started to speak to me in English! He said he used to live in Philadelphia. He told me he was twenty-nine years old and asked me if I thought he would die, and when I told him "No," he grabbed my hand and thanked me over and over again. Then he unpinned and gave me his aviator's badge — he said they would take it away from him anyway. I have it and shall keep it as a souvenir. I'll show it to you when I get back. Well, after I'd fixed him up, I saw that the observer had been wounded, too — shot just below the knee. It seemed funny to be giving first aid and trying to save their lives when just a minute or two before they had been shooting at us with their machine guns, trying to take our lives. But I consider that if I didn't do all I could to save them that I would be no better than they were. Of course a big crowd gathered in a few minutes and we sent the two aviators to the hospital in an ambulance, and under guard. As I said before, if they had been dropping bombs on some city and injuring innocent people, and I had got to them first, I would have shot them instead of giving them aid; but they were only shooting at us, and we are "fair game," so it was a fair fight, and they should be treated accordingly. Wish you could have been here and seen it — you may see it anyway because they took pictures of it all.

As before,
E. J. C[anright]

France
November 2, 1918

My dear Folks:

. . . As I have said before although I'm not afraid to die — I've seen too much of death to fear it — I don't *want* to die as I feel that I have the best part of my life before me. But that's my work, so I do it, and if I get "knocked off" why I will have the satisfaction of knowing that I've done my duty, anyways.

I can honestly say that I have had some of the happiest and also some of the bitterest experiences of my life since I have been a soldier. War is a great teacher and I have learned many lessons — some of them hard ones, too. You know I have actually seen what the Huns have done to northern France and Belgium and know what horrors and sufferings the people who lived there have gone through, and when things are going hard and I am tired and discouraged, I like to think that I am here going through all these hardships to do my bit to keep *you* all from experiencing the same horrors that these unfortunate people have — that if we don't lick the Huns now — and lick them to a *standstill* they might at some future time try to do the same thing in America. You can laugh at me if you want to, and say I'm foolish, but that thought gives me fresh determination to carry on. There is *nothing* I would not do to prevent you from going through even a part of what they have had to do. . . .

Love,

E. J. Canright

France

November 2, 1918

Dear Father —

. . . I feel like a slacker when I see those infantry — & the more I see them & hear of them, the more I feel a slacker. I've done all I can do, of course — happened to have the knowledge to put me where I am — & where I'd be more useful than in the infantry — & the rank — but the boys who are fighting the war are the doughboys — my hat is off to them. I get the backwash of war daily — sometimes am in the front — & often in the danger zone — but most of the time I am relatively safe — being an engineer officer, major, & topagraphical officer. It's not in my hands, naturally — but just the same I shall be loath to boast of my doings when the war is over — & neither am I going to make experiences by swimming into fire when my duties don't call me there — even the doughboy would despise that. Everybody who ever saw France will have tales to tell of their adventures — marvellous adventures — and, if the truth were known, most of them learned second hand. But the Infantry do endure Hell — danger, which is a good deal — & discomforts beyond descriptions — a whole lot more. But they get relieved — which our men haven't been since we came out here. . . .

Lots of Love
Affectionately
Vic [Morris]

France
September 22, 1918

Dear Anna:

. . . You can hardly imagine the immensity of effort in this war. I could waste reams of paper and not touch the high spots even. There is a sign "Look out for the cars" a few rods away written in three languages. I noticed today a Belgian, Canadian, French, Chinese, Senegalese, U.S. negro, and a Russian soldier. The troops of these classes mount to thousands and some to millions and we have said nothing of the British, Italians, Greeks, New Zealanders, So. Africans, Hindoos, Japanese, Australians each numbering thousands more and whose wealth and resources are being poured into this war. I have watched trucks loaded with soldiers pass for hours and hours. I have been where I could see and hear 80 cannon firing shells all day long and the least of these shells cost $12. I have seen captured German cannon that if harnessed up would fill all the streets of West Salem and make a long column out into the country. I dont know how many wrecked planes I have seen in odd places. I have seen 40 planes in one squadron. I have seen tanks lumbering by in strings. What I have seen is just a little part of the vast whole. It is tremendous, truly astounding. . . .

G. W. Garlock

"I'm not going to tell my mother what I have seen"

Fighting on the Western Front halted precisely at 11:00 A.M. on November 11, 1918. Soldiers had varied reactions as the war finally came to an end. The letters of Lyle Phillips, Kenneth White, and Harry Trippe, all written within a day of the Armistice, reveal the complex emotions experienced by Wisconsin soldiers. Feelings of euphoria and relief were mingled with horror on viewing the casualties from the final minutes of fighting, a desire to come home, and a quiet determination to continue with one's duties.

                                                                France
                                                       November 10, 1918
Dear Mother:
   Today I suppose is a great day of celebration in the United States
& in the whole world, I guess, except Germany. Official word of the
kaiser's abdication[25] & his sons resignations came last night, and
now it surely will be but a few hours before the guns will be silent. I
imagine you are getting rumor after rumor about conditions here.
We are, I know. Every little while someone hears it is all over, that
the armistice is signed. But we can tell when it really is over, (which
you can't) for we won't hear the guns nor see the flashes in the sky
any longer. Up to now they disprove every peace rumor we hear. . . .

                                                         Nov. 12, 1918.

   I was interrupted before I finished this letter, and since then so
much has been happening that I had no opportunity to resume.
   Yesterday I went up to the lines & did some work in what is left
of a nice little city. In the city when I arrived the artillery stationed
there was doing its share in a battle then going on a kilometer or so
away. I never heard such noise. Guns of all calibres were barking
away & over head the whirr of shells Germany-bound was almost
continuous. The whole town shook with the explosions. Then, precisely at 11 o'clock — I was sitting in a Salvation Army canteen
discussing doughnuts with a little Salvation Army girl from Minnesota, every thing stopped. The end of more than four years of war
had actually come. Not another shot was fired & since then all has
been quiet. At the hospital across the street from the canteen ambulance after ambulance continues to drive up and unload the poor
fellows who became casualties in that last few minutes of terrific
fighting. I went in among them as they lay there all bandage &
blood, and though some were very badly wounded, I didn't hear a
groan. Our boys sure are game.
   There has been a continuous ringing of church bells since yesterday. I was talking to an old French woman as the bells in this village
started to ring. Her face lit up, and she seized me by the hand and
said, "Ah, monsier mon lieutenant: Elles chantent a paix! Elles
chantent a paix!"[26]
   At our mess last night we had a special spread and the room all
decorated with French flags — we couldn't get American ones.

---

[25] On November 9, Kaiser Wilhelm II officially abdicated the German throne and fled to
Holland.

[26] "Ah, my lieutenant: They are singing peace! They are singing peace!"

Every one made a speech and "a lovely time was had." The little French woman in whose home we have our men couldn't understand a word of it, but she did understand the spirit of it, and sat by the stove and positively beamed. And she has had so much sadness in her face 'till now. . . .

With all the love in the world,

Your son,

Lyle

Limoges, France
November 12, 1918

Dear Mother, —

. . . When the French start a celebration they believe in doing a thoro job of it for they have been at it again all day today; Bells ringing, people parading, and everybody letting loose after four years of war. They are willing to give the Americans plenty of credit too for bringing the war to a speedy close. The American soldier stands ace high in France today.

While the French are busy celebrating the close of the war we are beginning to wonder how long it will be before we'll get started back home again. It is pretty hard to guess just now, but it looks as tho it would be several months yet at least. There are a great many things to be done here before we can come back and then we can't all come at once for it will take a great many shiploads to carry us all. If everything works smoothly tho, I expect to see the family again in April or May which is much sooner than I did when I started over here. . . .

With love,

Kenneth [White]

France
November 12, 1918

My precious Culla; —

. . . The armstice went into effect yesterday at 11:00 A.M. but the only way we can notice it is that we do not have to dodge the shells and can see a moonlight night, like tonight, without building up an "Abri" to crawl into when the Boche planes appear. No cheering or demonstration of any kind, everyone worked along at his job just the same as when we were sending every effort to get the heavies and the ammunition up to where they could send them over to the Huns. . . .

Always love
Harry M. Trippe

William Longhurst was born in Nekoosa, a community south of Wisconsin Rapids, in February, 1898. He moved with his family to Stevens Point as a young child and was graduated from Stevens Point High School in 1916. In the spring of 1917, Longhurst enlisted in the U.S. Army and served overseas as a private with Battery E of the 120th Field Artillery in the 32nd Division. When he returned to Stevens Point in 1919, Longhurst took a job with the Soo Railroad as a yard clerk. A few weeks later a tragic accident took his life just three months before his twenty-second birthday. Longhurst's letter to his father describes the euphoria of the French people at the time of the armistice.

France
November 24, 1918

Dear Father:

. . . I was in Paris the day that the Armistice was signed and believe me it sure was some live living. The people just threw aside every thing and just went out and celebrated. I never did see such a wild mob in all my life. Soldiers from all the Allied Nations were there on leave and the people sure did treat them royally. A man in uniform had a hard time to keep from being kidnapped by the French Madomosels and there sure was enough of them there to kidnap anybody. Nothing was any too good for a man in uniform no matter whether he was a French, English or American. I surely will never forget the time I had in Paris if I live to be a thousand years old. . . .

Your Loving Son
William

Although fighting along the western front stopped with the armistice, American troops remained in Europe until 1923. When the Treaty of Versailles was signed in June, 1919, 200,000 Americans remained in France. Like many veterans, Paul Lappley would soon return home, yet the scars of the "war to end all wars" would remain.

France
April 10, 1919

Dear Mother

. . . France sure is no place for an American boy. I havent started to drink yet and I leave the Mademoiselles alone, absolutely and I intend to keep it up as long as it may be my lot to stay here. I left home clean and will come back the same way.

There are still over a million of us over here and theyre going home fast, some day our turn will come, then we will shake off the mud and mire and hit the trail for home. We will try and forget some of the things we have seen and heard and bring back only the bright memories. I have seen and heard things which I never want to even hear mentioned again. As one Marine who was with the 5th U.S. Marines said to me. "Im not going to tell my mother what I have seen and gone through here in France and I never want to even hear them mentioned again." . . .

Sincerely
Paul

3

World War II

"A little trouble with Japan"

On December 7, 1941, Japanese forces attacked several American possessions in the Pacific Ocean. Although the American forces in the Philippines suffered serious damage, the most spectacular part of the attack occurred at Pearl Harbor, in Honolulu, Hawaii. American losses included the destruction of five battleships and damage to three other battleships, three destroyers, and three cruisers. On the nearby airfields, 180 planes were demolished and another 128 damaged. All told, almost 3,600 Americans were killed or wounded. On the following day, the U.S. Congress officially declared war on Japan.

Although the attack on Pearl Harbor had come as a surprise, preparations for possible American involvement in war had begun in 1940. In September of that year, President Franklin Roosevelt signed into law the nation's first peacetime draft, and the following month more than 16.5 million men registered with the Selective Service system. By 1945, out of a total military force of 8.3 million men and women, more than 7 million were draftees. In Wisconsin, 194,566 men were drafted between November, 1940, and September, 1945. All told, more than 16 million men and women served in the American armed forces during World War II, 332,200 of them from Wisconsin (including 9,000 women).

Sensing the coming war, twenty-one-year-old Richard I. Bong, of Poplar, in northwestern Wisconsin near Superior, had enlisted in the Army Air Corps on May 29, 1941. In December he was in training to become a fighter pilot. He wrote often to his mother, Dora Bong.

Luke Field
Phoenix, Arizona
December 8, 1941

Dear Mom,

Well It seems from the radio this afternoon that we are having a little trouble with Japan. A paper boy just came in and the Headlines say that Japan declared war on the U.S. Well that about

App. not req.

(LOCAL BOARD DATE STAMP WITH CODE)

Local Board No. 2   69
Dane County   025
MAY   4 1944   002
Room 263 Washington Bldg.
...........in

SELECTIVE SERVICE SYSTEM

Order to Report
Preinduction Physical Examination

4 May 1944
(Date of mailing)

The President of the United States,

To .... Harold .... Gustav .... Johnson .... 518 ....
   (First name)   (Middle name)   (Last name)   (Order No.)

GREETING:

You are hereby directed to report for preinduction physical examination at

.... 119 E. Wash. Ave., Rm. 307 ....
(Place of reporting)

at .... 5:15 A. .. m., on the .... 18th. .. of .... May .... , 194 4
(Hour of reporting)   (Day)   (Month)

(Member or clerk of Local Board)

E. N. Johnston, Clerk

IMPORTANT NOTICE TO REGISTRANT

Registrant who believes he has a disqualifying defect.—If you believe that you have some defect which will disqualify you for service you may, on or before the .... 10th. .. day of .... May .... , 194 4, appear in person at the office of the Local Board, or, if you are unable by reason of such defect to personally appear, you may submit an affidavit from a reputable physician or an official statement by an authorized representative of a Federal or State agency to the effect that such physician has personal professional knowledge or such authorized representative has official knowledge of your defect, the character thereof, and that you are unable to personally appear due to the character of the defect. The Local Board may send you to the Local Board examining physician, and, if it does so, it shall be your duty to appear at the time and place designated by the Local Board and to submit to such examination as the examining physician shall direct. If the Local Board determines that your defect does disqualify you for service you will receive a Notice of Classification (Form 57) advising you that you have been placed in Class IV–F. Unless prior to the date fixed for your preinduction physical examination, you receive such a Notice of Classification (Form 57) advising you that you have been placed in Class IV–F, you must report for your preinduction physical examination as directed.

Every registrant.—When you report for preinduction physical examination you will be forwarded to an induction station where you will be given a complete physical examination to determine whether you are physically fit for service. If you sign a Request for Immediate Induction (Form 219), and you are found qualified for service, you will be inducted immediately following the completion of your preinduction physical examination. Otherwise, upon completion of your preinduction physical examination, you will be returned to this Local Board. You will be furnished transportation and meals and lodgings when necessary. Following your preinduction physical examination you will receive a certificate issued by the commanding officer of the induction station showing your physical fitness for service or lack thereof.

If you fail to report for preinduction physical examination as directed, you will be delinquent and will be immediately ordered to report for induction into the armed forces. You will also be subject to fine and imprisonment under the provisions of section 11 of the Selective Training and Service Act of 1940, as amended.

If you are so far from your own Local Board that reporting in compliance with this order will be a hardship and you desire to report to the Local Board in the area in which you are now located, take this order and go immediately to that Local Board and make written request for transfer for preinduction physical examination.

DSS Form 215

16—37079-1   U. S. GOVERNMENT PRINTING OFFICE

WHi(X3)47100
Millions of American men received notices like this one, sent to Harold Johnson of Madison, directing them to report for a pre-induction physical. Courtesy Harold Johnson.

cinches the Christmas situation. We certainly won't get any time off now. We probably won't even get any time off on weekends. We will very likely be flying on weekends now and our graduation day may be set up a ways. . . .

Well the new order just came in. No One is to leave the post until further orders so I guess I won't need any civilian clothes for quite some time.

Well until I know more why keep your chin up and I'll help keep em flying.

Love
Dick

Born in Milwaukee in 1901, Stewart C. Yeo chose the army as his career in 1926. In 1941, Major Yeo was serving with the XI Corps Artillery, stationed in Hawaii with his wife, Eunice, and his children, Stewart ("Tuffy") and Mary Stewart. He wrote to his father, Fredric, describing the Japanese attack and its consequences.

Honolulu
December 15, 1941

Dear Dad:

I know you have read about the air raid of Dec. 7th. We are all safe and none the worse for the experience. The attack started at 7:55 A.M. Hawaiian time on Sunday morning. I was still in bed when the first bombs hit an airfield adjoining Schofield [Barracks]. After hearing a few more and machine gun firing above our quarters from planes I finally decided it must be the real McCoy. So I ran out in front with my field glasses and Eunice and Tuffy following. When we saw the large red spots, the rising sun, on the wings of the planes we only needed one guess. The Jap planes were flying around hither and thither machine gunning the area. Bullets went thru neighbors' houses and splattered the ground in front of the house. After retrieving Tuffy who broke away and ran out into the open across the street, we kept inside. A Jap bomber flew directly over where Eunice was standing at one time at a distance of about 100 feet, close enough to see the pilot. There were no casualties, miraculously, among the officers' dependents. I can give no information as to damage or casualties due to censorship. I reported immediately for duty at the Battalion and we moved to our defense station. Eunice and the kids were evacuated to the basement of concrete barracks until the morning raid was over and late that night they moved into the hills outside Honolulu, after the area was again machine gunned. The family stayed in Honolulu in a civilian cottage for 5 days and returned to Schofield. The maid, a loyal Jap, went with them. She is also a U.S. citizen by virtue of being born in Hawaii. Her name is Hisako Kusaka, but she is really a superior maid and was a great help to Eunice during this experience. There have been no attacks since the 7th, but one is enough with women and children around especially. The papers of course stress the attack on Pearl Harbor but the other points of attack: the airfields and adjoining areas had no picnic exactly. The forces are of course on constant alert and it is difficult to visualize the Japs trying anything here again. The Islands are under blackout every night. Martial law is in effect. Food and gasoline rationing is also in effect. I believe dependents will be sent home in the near future, altho nothing definite. We are going ahead with our Xmas celebration of course. I have not been home to see the folks since the raid but did see them twice under blackout after the kids were in bed while they were evacuees.

Best Regards from us all
Stewart

Twenty-two-year-old De Pere native Mark W. Smith had enlisted in the army in October, 1940, and was serving as a meteorologist with the 7th Air Corps Squadron in Kahuku, Hawaii, at the time of the attack. Corporal Smith wrote to his brother, Roger G. Smith, who was a student at the University of Wisconsin and who knew that he would soon be drafted.

Kahuku, Hawaii
December 24, 1941

Dear Lodger;

. . . Things are slowly returning to the semblance of normalcy here although many an eager eye is turned to the sky at the slightest provokation. No one seems to know or care that tomorrow is Christmas and it looks like festivities will be down to a minimum. I plan on being delt in on at least two big feeds but the usual sociability of the occasion will not be there, no drinks stronger than coke are available at present.

I suppose you are looking forward to the next draft with some compassion, I can't blame you feeling a little uneasy — it's nice to know whether you'll be home or a thousand miles away a month hence. My advice is to have as many good sprees as you can before the dye is cast because there is no longer much time for play in the Army. . . .

Your Brother,
Mark

The wedding of Roger G. Smith and Marcella Martinek in August, 1943.
Left to right: Mark W. Smith, Kitty Hogan, Roger Smith, Marcella
Martinek, Marcella's sister, and Margaret J. "Bene" Smith.
Courtesy Barbara Smith.

"Golly I look funny"

Entering the army meant a whole array of novel experiences for most
soldiers. The trip to a new part of the country for training often represented the first real voyage away from home. In addition, the recruits
were exposed to discipline of a sort they had never before encountered
and often were learning skills for which none of their previous experiences
had prepared them. Military uniforms — and military haircuts —
changed the way recruits looked. The military regimen was often impres-
sive. Roland Malcolm "Mac" Andresen commented on "the high morale
of the Marine Corps and the exceedingly high caliber of the officers. . . . I
am certain that the Marines aren't living on their reputation." David
Schreiner, a former football star at the University of Wisconsin, wrote,
"I'm really enjoying the Marine Corps although I had no idea that
discipline would be as strict as it has been. Our Corporal is a little king in
himself and we, his servants, do his every wish and command."

WHi(X3)39749

The 32nd Division in training at Camp Livingston, Louisiana, 1941.

John Jenkins, however, saw military training as somewhat unrealistic and incomprehensible. Jenkins grew up in Kenosha and was living in Madison and working as the museum director at the State Historical Society of Wisconsin when World War II began. He enlisted in June, 1942, and became an infantryman serving in the South Pacific and in Japan. Discharged from active service in December, 1945, Jenkins returned to the State Historical Society and worked there until 1954, when he became the head of the National Park Service's Western Museum. He died in 1964. This letter, describing his training experiences, was written to a former co-worker at the Society, Mary Foster.

Camp Wheeler, Georgia
September 27, 1942

Dear Miss Foster —

... We start the day at 5:45 AM and usually are busy until "lights out" at 9 PM. We've been especially busy the past two weeks, learning how to take apart, clean, and shoot three different types of rifles.

In between times we've drilled and been lectured at. Many of the lectures are in movie form — and I have a faint suspicion that these will be our only training in some phases of our military education.

So much time seems to be taken up with "dressed up" military courtesy that doesn't seem to have a place these days. For instance, we stand to (at attention) for 20 minutes each evening for Retreat, and usually we just barely have time to wash our hands and faces and change from work uniforms to our "kahki's." Then we have lectures on personal cleanliness! Of course, we are free to shower, shave, shine shoes etc. etc. after 9 PM! They're so generous.

I know I would appreciate more actual training — with the rifle, for instance, we shot 10 shots in each of four positions and then had to repeat that and qualify as marksmen. Needless to say I was one of the many who didn't qualify because many of us had never handled guns before in our lives. I could do all right in practice when I had all the time I needed, but when they rushed us my accuracy in aiming decreased.

It is quite different, this being thrown in with 59 strangers with no opportunity for privacy. Usually, as now, I write letters, sitting taylor fashion, on a hard steel locker with several conversations going on and a card or dice game also in progress.

There are recreational facilities in the Camp including 4 movie theaters, a library and bowling alleys, billiards, ping pong, etc. etc. Each battalion (about 4 companies of 250 men each) has a writing room in conjunction with a chaplain's office, but it seldom takes care of all the men who want to use it.

Just what my training will consist of I don't know. All that we do know is that we'll have 6 weeks of basic infantry training plus weeks of specialized Intelligence training — whatever that may be. Just what Infantry Intelligence means still remains a mystery to me. . . .

Sincerely
John Jenkins

Beaver Dam native Fred J. Draeger joined the navy in 1942. He trained at the Great Lakes Naval Training Station in Waukegan, Illinois, and was then sent to Memphis, Tennessee, for further instruction.

Memphis
October 30, 1942

Dear Friends:

. . . After completing, "Boot Training" at Camp Green Bay, I returned to the main station at the "Lakes," where I was placed in a unit awaiting school assaignment. I had been selected for Naval aviation ordnance training and when the call came through, I was transfered down here to Memphis.

Never having been in the South, I found it quite a revelation — I mean their manner of speech & peculiarities which make their mode of living. Then, too, their regard for the Negroe is all new & strange — I never have had anyone make such an unusually obvious effort at getting out of my way or take such special care not to touch or brush me in passing as these Tenn. negroes — Their lot if any must be small, in these sections.

It was interesting coming down here & finding the Civil War no longer being fought — The boys back at Great Lakes, had fed me that old line about "Yankees" being at a disadvantage in the South, so much, that I had almost begun to believe some of it. — True Southern Hospitality is quite in evidence around Memphis — As a matter of fact, the city and surrounding communities have gone far out of their way to extend the hand of friendship & good will; and whether it be refreshment, entertainment, or just plain service, all has been provided for — The servicemen really appreciate it. . . .

I remain — Respectfully
Freddy

Louis F. Rodey grew up on a farm in Sherman Township in Dunn County. He was drafted by the army in October, 1942, but by entering the reserves he obtained a deferment to finish the school year, entering the military in June, 1943. Rodey was sent to Europe in September, 1944, where he served as an infantryman and light machine gunner with Company G of the 324th Infantry Regiment, 44th Division, which fought in France and Germany and later moved into Austria. While fighting, Private Rodey was twice wounded, but he rejoined his unit after recuperating. Rodey returned to the United States in July, 1945, and was discharged from the army in November. He returned to Menomonie, finished his college education on the GI Bill, and worked as a physical plant superintendent at the University of Wisconsin-Stout until his retirement in 1985. Rodey wrote to his former high school teacher, Minda Dockar.

Camp Phillips, Kansas
July 9, 1944
Dear Mrs. Dockar,
I'm a bit late in thanking you and Miss Bates[1] for the birthday greetings. I guess I was home on furlough at the time. June 21st, my

[1] Hattie Bates, another of Rodey's former high school teachers.

birthday, I reported back here for duty. Under the circumstances, it was a happy birthday. Thanks a lot folks!

You know a furlough is a wonderful thing. While it's in effect, a guy feels likes to raise the roof, and when it's over, he feels like he has stumbled and the roof fell on top of him. From the time you know you're getting it, until the day you get back, your happiness pretty nearly follows a path described by the first 180 of the sine curve. Yes, exactly. You see folks, I haven't forgotten all I did learn back in school even though this infantry life does tend to make one thick between the ears. I could have used another 13 days very well. I didn't even get to see you folks, and I really did intend to.

We won't be here at Phillips much longer I'm sure, and I'd hate to predict where we might go. But there are rumors, and in the army, when rumors are persistant enough, well — it's true.

We spend a good share of our nites sleeping in the wide open spaces now. That G.I raincoat makes a marvelous bed too. Especially when it rains. If the army would only issue a foxhole with a leak proof roof; that would solve a great problem.

I'm in a machine gun section of a rifle company. Boy, if I could get home 1/10 of the ammunition we blast up, I could go deer hunting in Wisconsin every year for the rest of my life. That will be the day the one. I'll close for this time folks.

Sincerely,

Louie

As a result of the conflict, nearly 500,000 German and Italian prisoners of war were transported to the United States and kept there for the duration. German prisoners of war were kept in the U.S. from the beginning of the North African campaign in 1942 until mid-1946. Prisoners were housed in former Civilian Conservation Corps camps in the South and Southwest and at a number of military posts. Life for prisoners of war in the United States in many ways resembled that of American soldiers in camps. Days were filled with a variety of chores, and recreation and educational opportunities were offered. In addition, POWs found that the food surpassed that available in the war zone.

Milwaukee native Tom Boisclair was born in 1921 and was graduated from the University of Wisconsin in 1942. After going through basic training, the army sent Boisclair to George Washington University Medical School in Washington, D.C., from which he received his M.D. in 1947. Boisclair practiced medicine in Virginia until his death in 1983. While in Madison, he worked as a waiter at Ann Emery Hall, and he wrote to his supervisor there, Lillian Otto Fried.

Camp Hood, Texas
July 22, 1943

Dear Mrs Fried,

. . . Yipe, the other day I hit a new low. I had garbage detail. Now, that wasn't bad at all. I even got used to standing knee deep in the stuff, on the back of a great big truck. Oh boy, there were flys all over the place. Finally I could even sit down in the stuff and read the funnies that I found in the rubbish. I was beginning to enjoy it, for I thought of the rest of those poor guys out in the drill area working like a dog. Well here's the pay off. When we got to the place where we dump this garbage and burn it — ha, there was a whole stack of German prisoners doing the same darn thing. Hmmm, now I know how I stand. I guess they don't plan on making me a General for a long time — they certainly wouldn't treat me like that if they did.

These Germans are really good boys. I have a hunch that they're getting all of the Grade A food in this country. They certainly look healthy. They are all from the Africa Korps and still wear their uniforms when they work. They still have the German eagle on their hats. We were not suppose to talk to them and that went for their guards too. However the whole gang of us were doing everything but having a beer party. They talked English very well and use American slang like a college graduate. They think Hitler is a skunk and now use the Churchhill V for a salute in exchange for the nazi "sieg heil" — They were surprised to see that N.Y. was still standing, for they had heard that it had been bombed to bits. They also thought that the Japs controled our west coast. They have been here at Hood for a month and like it very much — yet five of them tried to escape about two weeks ago. They didn't get to 1st base. I finally have a genuine G.I. hair cut. They put the finger on me the other day. I did a pretty good job of stalling, but finally they got me. I was trapped. Golly I look funny. . . .

Best Regards,
Tom

Vivian Croake was born in 1911 in Janesville and was graduated from Janesville High School and Beloit College. When World War II started, she was working as a secretary for the Madison law firm of Thomas, Orr & Isaksen. In 1943, she enlisted in the Red Cross and served as a hospital recreation worker until February, 1946. She was stationed in Texas, Hawaii, Okinawa, and Korea. After the war, Croake returned to Madison, and in 1949 she married Charles Ward and moved to Philadelphia, where she still lives. Her letter was written to Herbert H. Thomas, San W. Orr, and Leon E. Isaksen.

Temple, Texas
January 31, 1944

Dear Mr. Thomas, Mr. Orr and Mr. Isaksen,

... The hospital is a huge place and the first day I was here I was sure I never would be able to learn my way around. I have been here one month and I still get confused in certain parts of the building, but I have my beaten path pretty well under control. . . . Wards 115 and 116 are Malaria wards and Ward 117 is mostly arthritis. Of course, all of my malaria cases are victims of the South Pacific and I can add that everyone of them is glad to be back in the States and the majority feel that they have done their part and would just as soon get out of the Army. They think anyone is crazy who wants to go overseas. The Army is not discharging anyone for malaria alone. Most of the patients when recovered enough to leave the hospital are sent to some camp near their home as instructors or whatever capacity they are fitted for. A lot of them haven't been home for two or three years and they can't wait to get out of the hospital. . . . The boys seem to be very bitter about the fact that civilians are taking the war so casually and that it is necessary to have victims of this war go around and talk to war bond rallys to get the people to subscribe. I can't say that I have talked to anyone who thought that overseas assignment was thrilling though a lot of them say that if they are sent back to duty they would rather be in the thick of things than to be sent to some camp here doing routine work. It is really quite heartrending to see a whole gang of fellows coming along in wheelchairs and on crutches. If more people could visit this hospital they certainly would become conscious of the horrors of war. . . .

There are Italian and German prisoners here. Every Monday the Italian prisoners cook their own dinner in the kitchen on their ward. I was invited as a guest one night and the Captain immediately adopted me as his name was Captain Viviano and he got quite a kick out of my name being Vivian. Outside of that time I have only been in the prisoners wards twice. I think most of them are glad to be here and I think they feel that is is too good to be true and keep expecting something horrible to happen to them eventually. The Captain has learned quite a bit of English since he has been here so I told him all about Wisconsin and education in the United States. Our first course, which I thought was the main one, was a great heaping dish of spaghetti. I only ate about half of mine and was

stuffed and then they brought a piece of steak and salad. For dessert
I had an apple. . . .

Sincerely,
Vivian

Europe/Africa

By the time of the U.S. entry into the war, fighting had been raging in
Europe for more than two years. In December, 1941, Germany controlled
most of continental Europe, and fighting was taking place in North Africa, where Field Marshal Erwin Rommel and his famous Afrika Korps
operated, and on Germany's eastern front, where Russian and German
troops were locked in combat. In Great Britain, American troops joined
the Allied forces in preparation for an invasion of Europe.

In July and August, 1943, Allied forces retook Sicily, and beginning in
September, 1943, they fought on the Italian peninsula itself. Finally, on
June 6, 1944 (D-Day), the Allies invaded France. From that day on,
Allied troops marched eastward and northward toward Germany, while
troops from the Soviet Union advanced from the east. On April 30, 1945,
Adolf Hitler killed himself in his Berlin bunker. When word of his death
reached the German troops, virtually all resistance to the Allied onslaught
ended. On May 7, German General Alfred Jodl signed surrender documents to go into effect at 11:01 P.M. on May 8. The war in Europe had
ended.

"It was here that I got my first taste of those lovable pup tents."

Virtually all of the men and women serving in Europe were undergoing
an entirely new experience. The vast majority had never seen combat
before, and most had never visited Europe or Africa. As William L.
Schlicher wrote, "What I have seen of Africa appears to me as very
strange and also a little weird." In addition, the military imposed strict
censorship regulations about what soldiers could include in their letters.
Many subjects — some of them seemingly unimportant — could not be
discussed. As a result, letters home often included only general observations on subjects like food, the country the letter was written from (although without giving specific location), and other living conditions.
These letters provide insights into the American soldier's way of life.

As a young adult, Roy F. Bergengren, Jr., moved to Madison, where
his father was one of the founders of CUNA credit union. Bergengren
worked at the *Wisconsin State Journal* in Madison for five years before
enlisting in the army in 1941. He served as an aircraft controller with the
311th Fighter Control Squadron, 63rd Air Defense Wing, and with the
78th Fighter Control Squadron, 2nd Air Defense Wing, rising to the rank
of major. By the time of his discharge in 1945, Bergengren had seen
action in England, Africa, Sicily, Italy, France, and Germany. After the
war, he received an M.A. and Ph.D. from the University of Florida and

also taught at that institution. He served as president of Daytona Beach Community College for fourteen years and died in 1982 at the age of sixty-seven. He wrote to Don Anderson and other co-workers at the *Wisconsin State Journal.*

North Africa
1943

Dear Roy, Mac, Don, et al,

. . . I've had a very interesting little trip and I could sure write some damn fine P-1 Sunday features, but alas, this must go through the censor. Right now I'm holed up in Africa (where I cannot say) and am a busy little boy. My duties (I'm not allowed to describe them) are fascinating. The food — I can't describe that either. But the weather is wonderful. No more of that English raw rain. I gladly gave up the luxuries of RAF life for a bit of sunshine.

Captain Roy F. Bergengren, Jr. Courtesy Rosemary Bergengren.

WHi(X3)47091

I've seen most of Britain and threw away a lot of cold cash in London. I also had a fine trip to "the Rock" [of Gibraltar]. I'll tell you all about it before too long — I hope. I miss my wife, but that's only natural, isn't it? My physical condition is excellent. And my financial condition, I fear, is static since "there ain't no promotion this side of the ocean" unless one is damn lucky which I'm not. . . .

Love and kisses,

Bergie

John Warren was born in 1898 in Tomah. He served in France during World War I and then moved to California, where he became a well-known artist with Disney Studios. During World War II, he became a Red Cross field director with the 90th Division, serving on Omaha Beach during the D-Day invasion and in France and Czechoslovakia with General George Patton's 3rd Army. In November, 1946, Warren was awarded the Medal of Freedom (the highest honor available to civilians) for exceptional meritorious and untiring service to front-line troops, often under enemy fire. After the war, he returned to Madison, where he worked as a counselor at the University of Wisconsin and taught art classes. He died in October, 1979. His letters are to his wife, Elizabeth.

England

April 22, 1944

Darling:

. . . Our principal recreation here is visiting the pubs of an evening. Our favorites are the small neighborhood pubs, which presumably have been serving son, father, and grandfather, and so on back to the dawn of time. It is a rare occasion when one gets a drink of Scotch. Sometimes *one* bottle is produced of an evening, and when it is gone there is no more. About the same scheme of things applies to gin, we find the "bitter" pretty good stuff, and sometimes there is plenty of Guinness Stout, although any and everything is apt to run out in the course of evening. Pubs open at 6 PM and close at 10, so the evening is soon gone.

We are all practising "darts". Some of the British are suprisingly good; many are no better than most of us. I've played quite a few games, a native and a Yank pairing up against one or more similar pairs. We are always careful to have some of the natives playing — unless they insist our playing among ourselves — in order that they will not feel we have preempted what must be, for many, their sole pastime. Without exception everybody has been very friendly. It is soon Bill, and John, and Alf. They love to sing in one of our favorite — and one of the smallest — pubs, and sing almost exclusively

American songs, knowing verse after verse, which is more than can be said of us. . . .

Love,
J

In 1942, at the age of twenty, Russell Barr, of Madison, enlisted in the army. Barr, a private first class, served with the 87th Infantry Division as an ammunition carrier in England, France, Belgium (the Battle of the Bulge), and Luxembourg. After his discharge in August, 1945, Barr worked for Wisconsin Bell in Janesville. He died on June 18, 1991. He wrote to his parents, Mr. and Mrs. Elmer Barr.

England
October 26, 1944

Dear Mom & Dad;
Just a line to tell you that I am OK and I'm in England. It is cold and damp here and I have a cold naturally. The quarters here are poor, but I guess they are just as good comparatively as the average Englishman's home. There were negros here a few months ago and they told us that the English girls went with them the same as with any other soldiers. Some of them are even going to have babies from them. That sure lowered my opinion of the English people. I am mailing this as it may get there faster than free mail. But I think I'll write free mail from now on as I can't write enough on this. Believe it or not I am wearing long underwear as there is no heat in this building. It isn't all wool thou. The country is pretty, but I am still glad and thankful to be an American.

Love, Russ

Carl Schluter was born in Madison on August 31, 1921. In 1942, he was working as an apprentice printer at the *Wisconsin State Journal* when he was drafted. Schluter joined the 28th Infantry Division as an infantryman with the rank of sergeant and was first sent to England and then to France in July, 1944. His unit fought at Ouren, Belgium (near where Belgium, Luxembourg, and Germany meet), when the German assault struck the American lines in December, 1944. The 28th Division was virtually destroyed in the ensuing Battle of the Bulge. After his discharge in September, 1945, Schluter returned to Madison and his work at the *Wisconsin State Journal*. He now lives in Fairchild, near Eau Claire.

Don Anderson, the publisher of the *State Journal*, periodically sent many former staffers serving in the armed forces a newsletter with updates on the activities of their colleagues. Anderson also created a savings account for each former staff member into which the *State Journal* deposited $15.00 each month, so that they would each have a nest egg when discharged. Finally, every year Anderson sent each staffer a Christmas package containing such things as a pocket knife, food, or, one year, a

15 October 1944
[2 yrs in army today]

Dear Margaret —

Almost all the mail again, but *sniff*!

From an inundated soldier, greetings and grateful thanks. I've spent free time (*when?*) this week plowing thoroughly through the Times and magazines; read the Derleth poems and the detective or mystery anthology; loaned out the poetry books; and shall soon get to the Derleth novel. Think I'll save Westward, Ho! for a movement eastward — unless

WHi(X3)47099

For soldiers far from their families, mail was highly valued, as Sergeant Gordon Petersen of Milwaukee expressed in this drawing in a letter to Margaret Reynolds, a former co-worker at First Wisconsin National Bank. Petersen died in March, 1945, of wounds received in action in France.

pinup calendar. Because of the unreliability of the mail, the packages would be mailed in October and would arrive any time between November and the following May or June. In 1944, the package included some Wisconsin cheese.

Belgium
December 5, 1944

Dear Mr. Anderson,

. . . We had a nice feast out of the cheese. We saved some bread from chow and with the beer we obtained, through proper channels of course, we spent the night in good old Fauerbach Brewery style.[2] By the way, I'm in Belgium now but the beer was from Luxembourg. The people from Luxembourg are really the brewers of beer I understand; anyways they're tops as far as I'm concerned. Its wonderful tasting but its not very potent, about one half of one per cent I hear. The French and Belgians are not to[o] hot at beer making but I'll take their wine, its really beautiful stuff. Had quite a bit of it while moving through their countries but we moved to[o] darn fast.

Sort of a nice peaceful night tonight, just routine patrol duty. Occasionally some Jerry opens up with his "Burp" gun, don't know whether he's calling someone or not but he gets plenty of answers. Beautiful sounding, those .30 caliber machine guns. Occasionally we get a bracket of artillery but nothing to worry about; thats getting to be routine too. But they'd better cut that stuff out, someone's liable to get hurt. . . .

Respectfully,
Sgt. Carl Schluter

Four days before his twenty-first birthday, on January 13, 1942, Warren Radke, an apprentice in the composing room at the *Wisconsin State Journal*, enlisted in the Army Air Forces. Radke attained the rank of staff sergeant and was attached to the 60th Fighter Squadron, 33rd Fighter Group as an airplane mechanic. In this capacity he served in Africa, Pantelleria (an Italian island in the Mediterranean), Italy, India, China, and Burma before receiving his discharge in June, 1945. After a six-month courtship, he married Dorothy Fiore on December 1, 1945. After the war, Radke returned to the *Journal*, where he finished his apprenticeship and became the composing room night foreman until he died of cancer on September 9, 1955. Radke was awarded a Purple Heart for wounds received during an enemy bombardment on February 7, 1943. Throughout his tour of duty, Radke wrote to Don Anderson at the *Journal*.

[2] A Madison brewery that operated from 1868 until 1966.

North Africa
June 29, 1943

Dear Mr. Anderson —

. . . Now that the African campaign is over I'm going to try and tell you everything. We landed at Casablanca but it's not what it's cracked up to be. We were there only a few days and we flew up to "Andja," French Morocco. It was here that I got my only real bath in a bath tub with all the hot water I wanted. We must have been in the tub half a afternoon and to think we thought we were dirty then. It was here that I got my first taste of those lovable pup tents.

From here we took a troop train up to Telergma, Algeria and this place really stunk. All we saw was mud and it seemed like it rained continually.

We were here a very short time and then flew to Yaukes les Bains[3] on the Tunesian border. It is located high in the mountains and all it is, is some old Roman ruins with a few Arabs thrown in. I bathed in some old Roman baths with water from a hot spring but very hard. This place was a hot spot deluxe for us the first evening there (I didn't even have my tent pitched) and all hell broke loose. German Ju88's,[4] I don't know how many really let lo[o]se. We were on a slight knoll and those bombs hit all around the knoll and me without a trench to crawl into. That night I guess I was scared — I just lay down and hoped to God I'd live to be back in Madison. We had numerous raids (daylight) after that until my fatal day.

One late morning I was replacing a hydraulic selector valve in the cockpit when out of the sun came our friends. I didn't see them in time but I was out and running. There was one particular Folke Woulf[5] I didn't notice and he zoomed right over me and let loose. The concussion picked up and I landed on my face and laying there I noticed my right leg wasn't functioning. Well the ambulance picked me up and three days later I was moving around. My plane looked like a sieve and it was junked. I also had a small bit of shrapnel in my left leg and my back. . . .

Warren Radke

"Into the jaws of a hell"

The war experience exposed millions of young men and women to fear and death on a scale they could never before have known. During the

[3] Youks-les-Bains, about 250 miles southeast of Algiers.
[4] Junkers Ju88, a twin-engine German bomber.
[5] Focke-Wulf Fw190, a single-engine German fighter plane.

war, the United States had 407,316 soldiers killed and another 670,846 wounded. Nearly 8,000 men and women from Wisconsin lost their lives in the conflict, while 13,600 from the state were wounded. Carl Schluter, John Miller, John Warren, and Le Roy "Whitey" Holm gave particularly good voice to the emotional side of the war.

When Schluter wrote this letter to Don Anderson, he was a veteran of six months of bloody fighting in France and Belgium. He could not know that in less than one month the Germans would launch the counteroffensive known as the Battle of the Bulge.

Belgium
November 19, 1944

Dear Mr. Anderson,

I hardly know how to begin after such a long time and I really have been sweating it out.

But speaking of sweating things out, in the past two weeks there was a few mornings that really called for a good deal of sweating out. It used to be fairly peaceful to lay in our foxholes but these particular mornings there was plenty of big stuff falling nearby. I never was too scared of the stuff until then. We happened to be about eight miles inside of Reich and the artillery was coming from all directions. Everytime a shell started to whistle in, I was beginning another prayer. As one of the 'doughfeet' put it, "I may not get the Purple Heart for being wounded but if they give them out for being scared as hell I certainly rate one," and that's no kiddin'. . . .

Respectfully,
Carl Schluter

John R. "Jack" Miller was a Madison native who had joined the Royal Canadian Air Force in May, 1941, before the U.S. entry into World War II. In May, 1942, he was in the process of being transferred to the American Army Air Forces when he met his future wife, Elaine, on a blind date. They had five more dates and were married on June 1, 1942.

Miller piloted a B-17 heavy bomber from May, 1943, until early 1944, when he returned to the United States. He was discharged from active duty in October, 1945, and remained in the reserves until 1957. Miller also worked as a pilot and flight instructor and later went into sales before his retirement in 1972.

In June, 1943, Captain Miller was a lead pilot stationed with the 8th Air Force's 95th Bomb Group in England. On June 13, the group went on its ninth mission (Miller's third), a bombing raid over Kiel, Germany. The aircraft encountered heavy resistance, and twenty-six of the sixty planes involved in the raid were shot down, ten of them from Miller's squadron of eighteen bombers. The men killed in the raid included Miller's roommate and other close friends. He wrote to Elaine telling her of the previous day's carnage. Because Miller had gone through training with many of the men killed, his wife had become friendly with their wives.

England
June 14, 1943

Dearest Elaine;

Darling I am sorry I haven't had time to write you. I consider you are very lucky, tho — Because I am still here, and I love you very much. I have lost very many friends, Elaine is why I consider you lucky. Harry S., Walter Thisann, Don Scaratto, and Maj. Wilder were shot down yesterday. We have lost alot — Elaine, dont say anything to the girls until they say something to you. I am not feeling very well after yesterday. I'll tell you all about it some day if you want to hear, but I'd rather not talk about it and especially write about it. I have a souvenir of yesterday's battle — I'll show it to you soon. Please dont worry about me because I'm O.K. and will be. You will have me when I come, that is more than some people will have.

Elaine, I love you and always will. Remember that — If I dont write for several days you will know that I have been busy. I am always thinking of you sweetheart —

Love, Jack!

In April, 1944, Red Cross Field Director John Warren wrote to his wife, Elizabeth, describing how he had been playing darts and singing songs in English pubs. Three months later, he had moved into France after the invasion of Normandy, and his view of the war had changed dramatically.

France
July 22, 1944

Darling:

. . . Yesterday I had to visit all the units again, to get statements for my report. The regiment is in contact with the enemy, so such trips always have their skin-prickling moments. I got back pretty tired about 7 o'clock, just in time to get a phone call from the CO of one of Sirrine's battalions, also in the line, requesting me to come up to discuss personal problems of his body-guard, a fine young fellow who had simultaneously received word that his sister, an Army nurse, and a brother, a flyer, had both been killed in the So. Pacific, and that his remaining brother had been critically wounded with another division here in France.

While up there, I hit the favorite hours for Jerry's activities, and, frankly, pretty nearly had the pants scared off me, with samples of shelling, mortar-fire, and strafing. I got back at midnight, having driven the jeep myself all day (my driver being on guard) slipping and slewing through mud axle deep whenever I got off the surfaced roads, which was frequently. I hate to admit it, but after a day like that, I feel my years. Yeah, man! War is a young man's game! . . .

News on 90th has been released. Maybe you know something now of what the boys have gone through: constant contact with the enemy since D-Day. They've taken their losses, too. Somebody says "Old Bill got it today." "No!" you say. "Son-of-a-bitch!" And you go on about your business, with a little more emptiness inside, a little more tiredness, a little more hatred of everything concerning war.

There is a certain cemetery where some of my closest friends in the Division lie. I saw it grow — shattered bodies lying there waiting for graves to be dug. Now it is filled. The graves are neat and trim, each with its cross. Occasionally I visit it when passing by. Always there are flowers on the graves: Sometimes a potted geranium has been newly brought in; sometimes there is a handful of daisies. The French people, and especially the children, seem to have charged themselves with this little attention.

Our bombers are roaring overhead just now, in the hazy afterglow of sunset. In a few seconds I'll hear the crunch of bombs — a good-night kiss for the Nazis. There they go!

The war news is good; but we're fighting over optimism. I suppose people at home are elated; the boys up front are still in their fox-holes.

I'll try to write at least a note every day or so. Take care of yourself. I'm fine.

Love,
John

In 1941, Le Roy "Whitey" Holm was a high school teacher in Sparta, in Monroe County. He enlisted in the army before the war started and became a major in the inspector general's office, responsible for solving problems with antiaircraft guns. After his discharge in 1946, Holm attended the University of Wisconsin and obtained a doctoral degree in botany and biochemistry. He later became a professor at the U.W.

Holm had studied at La Crosse State Teachers College, where one of his history teachers was Myrtle Trowbridge. In February, 1945, the Allied forces in northern Europe, where Holm was stationed, were preparing to begin their offensive into Germany itself, slogging around in mud and burying ammunition so that Nazi airplanes couldn't bomb it. Holm's duties also included unloading trucks that returned from the front laden with the frozen bodies of dead soldiers "stacked like cordwood," among

WHi(X3)47081
Medics carrying a wounded soldier near Holstam, Germany, in February, 1945. Signal Corps photo.

them large numbers of officers. As he carried ammunition, Holm listened to enlisted men taking out their frustrations on the officers, claiming that they had it easy during the war. Having seen the corpses of other officers who had given their lives in the fighting, Holm felt that officers should be defended, so, as he put it, "I unloaded my heart to Miss Trowbridge."

Holland
February 22, 1945

Dear Miss Troby,

. . . But the gents that I speak of down here are usually known but to a few — and ask no publicity. They are some of the officers and NCOs who live down there in hell — just a few miles from here —

and they stay there days, weeks, and months, until they are killed. There are just a few. They teach men, feed them, protect them, clothe them, comfort them, cheer them, and lead them sooner or later into the jaws of a hell that is the bloodiest, dirtiest, most vicious kind of murder that man, with all his machines, has been able to devise.

These men are loved with a kind of love that exists no place but on the battlefield — and it is never talked about. These gents go for days without sleep, give away their clothes, go without food, keep going when they are sick, perform miraculous feats when they are wounded, and take the suicidal details rather than ask someone else to do it. They are never afraid, they are never cold, they never complain, and they spend all of their time trying to think of ways to help their men — and to save them. I don't know if they are happy — but if it isn't selflessness I never hope to see it.

And I don't mean to leave out the privates — but the officers and non-coms are the ones I'm thinking of. Remember I said there were just a few like this. The stories come trickling in every once in a while. They usually stay there until they die. Surely they must be God's people. He was like that. I'm sure they swore and drank and did a lot of other things — but I am sure God got them when they went away. . . .

Bye you,
Whitey

"Too horrible to even try and imagine": Liberation of Prisoners of War and Concentration Camps

Approximately 95,000 Americans — mostly airmen and ground troops — became prisoners of war in the European theater during World War II. To house their captives, the Germans built an extensive network of more than seventy-five camps and hospitals throughout Germany, Poland, Czechoslovakia, and Austria. Although conditions in these camps were theoretically regulated by the Prisoner of War Code of the Geneva Convention, signed in 1929, American soldiers often received poor treatment, a situation that angered their countrymen. On seeing one of the camps in Germany, Bernard J. Kennedy wrote, "Time will make [the Germans] pay for what they have done. They should be made to pay for it by the end of a rifle or something."

Walter Keenan and Paul Fergot were two of the men from Wisconsin who became prisoners. Keenan was born in 1910 and grew up in Stoughton. As a member of the reserves, the army activated him in 1941. Captain Keenan, an infantry soldier, was taken prisoner in Europe in September, 1944, and was held at Oflag 64, a camp for ground force officers about 150 miles northwest of Warsaw, Poland. In February, 1945, the Germans evacuated the camp because Russian forces were nearing the area. The prisoners were forced to march 150 miles west to the Stalag III A camp at Luckenwalde, Germany, from which camp Keenan was liberated by the Russians in May, 1945. He came home to the United States a month later and subsequently served in occupied Japan from 1950 to 1952. He retired from the army with the rank of lieutenant colonel in 1960 and died in Milwaukee in 1966. He wrote to his parents, Dr. and Mrs. H. A. Keenan, of Stoughton.

Paul L. Fergot was born in 1922 in Embarrass, near Shawano, and grew up in Wautoma. He was a student at Oshkosh State Teachers College, but because he was about to be drafted, he enlisted in the Army Air Forces in November, 1942, less than three months after marrying the former Loa Hutchins. Fergot was a navigator whose plane was shot down over northern Italy on October 10, 1944. On October 25, Loa received a telegram informing her that Paul was missing in action. Loa was attending Oshkosh State Teachers College at the time, and her parents read the telegram and came to the school to give her the news. As she recalled, "I saw my folks walking down the hall. I knew right away what had happened, so . . . I just slid down to the floor and sat there for a long time. . . . Then my dad got down next to me and he said, 'He's only missing, you know, so there's lots of hope yet.' . . . I can remember not wanting to do anything or think or move even." On November 5, Major General Nathan Farragut Twining sent Loa a letter that read, in part, "I am sorry that I can not give you any assurance of the safety of your husband" and went on to describe the circumstances under which he was shot down and to inform her that Paul had received several commendations, including the Purple Heart.

Paul landed safely, however, and remained in hiding with Italian partisans until December 18, when he decided to turn himself in to the Germans rather than risk being captured and executed. His wife, however, received no further information about him until March, 1945, when a message from Paul was broadcast over shortwave radio as part of a German propaganda transmission. The broadcast was audible only in the eastern United States, so Loa learned that her husband was safe because more than 100 people who heard the broadcast — people she did not know — from Florida to Vermont called her and sent her telegrams and postcards with Paul's message that he was a prisoner at Stalag Luft I, near Barth, Germany, and that he was safe. Shortly thereafter, Loa received official notification from the army of Paul's capture.

On May 27, Loa received another telegram from the military informing her that Paul was free. He had been liberated by the Russians on May 1 and had been transported with other former prisoners to Reims, France, by a squadron of B-17 bombers that evacuated more than 9,200 prisoners from the camp over two days. On June 24, Paul and Loa were reunited in Milwaukee, and for Loa, "It seemed like my life was beginning again."

Paul was deactivated on October 21, 1945, and served in the reserves until 1955. He finished his education at the University of Wisconsin and worked as an engineer in Oshkosh, where he and Loa still live.

Together, these two sets of letters provide good insight into the life of a prisoner of war and demonstrate the urgency that these men felt to get home and be reunited with their loved ones.

Oflag 64
Altburgund, Poland
December 31, 1944

DEAR MOTHER AND DAD —

HAVE SNOW TODAY. NOT TOO COLD THOUGH. MAKES ME HOMESICK TO SEE IT. RAN INTO AN OFFICER FROM JANESVILLE LAST NIGHT. ALMOST LIKE SEEING SOMEONE FROM HOME. HOPE YOU ALL HAD A NICE XMAS. I WAS THINKING OF YOU THAT DAY MORE THAN USUAL. SHOULD HAVE SOME MAIL IN A FEW WEEKS NOW. SEEMS A LONG TIME SINCE SEPT. WHEN I WAS TAKEN. AM GLAD 44 IS ALMOST DONE. HOPE 45 WILL SEE US ALL TOGETHER AGAIN. HAD A PRETTY GOOD MEAL ON XMAS. WAS ALMOST FILLED UP FOR ONCE. FELT STRANGE. HOPE THOSE FOOD AND TOBACCO PACKAGES ARE ON THE WAY FROM BER.[6] THEY WILL BE WELCOMED WITH OPEN ARMS. STILL READING A GOOD DEAL. HAVE AN EXCELLENT LIBRARY HERE. ITS A GOOD PASTIME. TAKE CARE OF YOURSELVES. HERES TO '45 —

LOTS LOVE WALT

Stalag Luft I
Barth, Germany
March 19, 1945

My Dearest —

It seems ages since I have heard from home. I certainly hope and pray that everything is alright there. There is so little to write about here. Just eating — sleeping — Reading — playing cards, e.t.c. It's beginning to get on my nerves. I'd give anything to hear from home, but don't dare to even hope for any thing for another couple of months. Honey, I'd like to ask you again, if you feel when you get this that it is practical, to send whatever parcels the Red Cross allows and if you send a food parcel to include plenty of chocolate and all things as condensed as possible — such as — Bisquick — Buckwheat — Pancake flour — jams — nuts — fruit cake e.t.c. perhaps some dried fruits. — Use your own judgement about it all, as I hope you are doing about everything at home. — You must take care of everything and everybody, Darling. Keep everything going as usual and soon we'll all be together again. Write to Howie &

6 Keenan's wife, Bernice.

WHi(X3)47090

Above: *Roll call at Stalag Luft I, the German prison camp in which Paul Fergot (circled) was held.* Below: *Mail was vital to those in prison camps. In addition to news of home, prisoners also requested that their families send food to augment the meager diet provided by their captors. Courtesy Paul and Loa Fergot.*

WHi(X3)47093

Janet & Gordon & Bill[7] for me and tell the folks I'll write to them again as soon as I can. Missing you more than you know, Dearest, I am still your lover & husband —

Paul

May 9, 1945

Dear Folks.

Am a free man the hard way. Will explain when I see you which should be in a few short weeks now. Was in Luckenwalde 30 mi from Berlin (S). I am well and needless to say quite happy. Crossed into the American Lines last night. Will you call Ber when you get this. I wrote her too, but in case she doesn't get it. Will call her as soon as I can after getting to the U.S. Being a P.W is no bed of roses. Am hungry after soup & spuds for so long. See you soon

Love Walt

France
May 20, 1945

Dearest Loa,

Still here in France, and will be for another ten days, I guess. I don't know for sure what's holding us up; ships, processing or what; But that's the way it is. I think I ought to be home before June 25th though. That'll make it about an even year since I was home last, huh? Mighty long time! Honey, I just don't know what to say. I know so little about what is going on & has gone, at home. I guess I'll just have to wait 'til I hear from you. — I sure hope I can get you by phone when I hit the states!

And by the way, Punkin, don't pay any attention to all the stories in magazines, etc, about the returning boys being strangers & having to be re-adapted and How to treat them, etc. — They're just the same, and they want the folks at home to be just the same too. So

---

[7] Howard Fergot (Paul's brother), Janet Hutchins (Loa's sister), Gordon Johnson (a friend of Paul's from Wautoma High School), and Bill Fell (a friend of Paul's from Oshkosh State Teachers College).

don't be worrying about how to treat me, or any such thing, Just pretend I'd never left — and I'll do the rest! I Love You Sweets,

Paul

France
June 10, 1945

Sweetheart,

Went to church tonite. Was delighted again to see colored & white boys worshipping together. I sure hope some of the principles of democracy learned in the army will carry on after the war. — Boy am I messing this up! — Poor Pen! Dont know if it'll last through this letter or not.

Wish I knew how you're making out, Honey. — New Pen — If I'd known I would be here this long, I'd have managed to get an answer some how. But they keep telling us — "You have to be out by June first" and such stuff — However, if the latest rumor developes, I'll be on my way on the 13th and in the states by the 20th

I think of you so much, Honey & wonder how you are, what you are doing, etc. It makes it hard to write not knowing a thing about home.

Some one on the radio is singing "Always." — I will be loving you always, Dearest. And right now, I'm wanting you so much I can hardly stand it. — Be with you soon though. — By the way, things change pretty rapidly in the army, but right now the War Dept. says Ex P.W.'s won't be deployed to the Pacific — and that suits me. — See you soon, sweets — Loads of Love Always. In fact, all my Love always!!

Paul

Fond du Lac native Kenneth E. Worthing was a lawyer who had served in the army reserves since 1929 and was activated in July 1941. After training in military government, he was commissioned as a colonel and sent overseas as the military government head for the XV Corps, which was attached at different times to both the 3rd Army and the 7th Army. In this capacity, he participated in the liberation of several prisoner-of-war camps, and he wrote home to his wife, Ruth, describing what he had seen. Discharged in October, 1945, Worthing practiced law in Fond du Lac until his retirement in 1970. He died in 1982.

Paul and Loa Fergot in Miami Beach during the late summer of 1945, shortly after they were reunited. Paul is quite thin as a result of poor nutrition during his captivity. Courtesy Paul and Loa Fergot.

Charmes, France
September 18, 1944
. . . Yesterday Bing Crosby's U.S.O. show was here. He really had a good show, and the G.I.'s went for it in a big way. Bing has a good personality and the show was much better than Dinah Shore's which I saw a few weeks ago.

We had quite an experience some time ago. We knew of an internment camp in which there were a lot of British and Americans. The general told me to get there as soon as possible to see that the people were treated all right, and not in danger, etc. We spent all day trying to reach the place and would get held up one place or another by road blocks. We finally got in with a cavalry group headed in that direction, but they quit about five miles away and we had to drive in the rest of the way in our jeep in the middle of the night going through territory we didn't know what to expect, no lights and planes constantly overhead. It was really quite a ride; I wasn't half as scared of the Germans as I was of the French who are out in organized bands looking for Germans. We were stopped half a dozen times by them, and you should have heard me trying to explain who we were. I regretted many times not having taken more interest in language studies in school.

We got to the place about 11:30 and were they glad to see us. We were the first Americans. Some of these people had been interned several years. They all felt that now we were there they should pack up and leave at once, and I am afraid that perhaps I became somewhat unpopular trying to convince them that though we came as liberators they had to wait until the roads were cleared of Germans and of military traffic, and that we had other things to do, besides load them up on our trucks and send them back by the first plane or boat to America or England. . . .

In addition to the network of camps for Allied prisoners of war, the Nazis also established a series of internment camps for civilian detainees from parts of occupied Europe. The most famous of these are, of course, the death and concentration camps in which millions of Jews, Catholics, gypsies, homosexuals, and other "undesirables" were killed. The largest and most notorious of these camps, like Auschwitz, were located in Poland and were liberated by Russian soldiers advancing westward; but smaller camps also existed, and it was one of these, in southwestern Germany, that Worthing describes in the following letter. Although the details of the Nazis' "Final Solution" are now well known, in 1944–1945

Allied soldiers had little idea of the horrors that were taking place inside
these camps.

> Sarrebourg, France
> January 1, 1945
>
> . . . I have been through a German prison camp. Frankly I
> thought some of these tales we had heard were exaggerated. This
> one was on top of a mountain. It has a couple of rows of barbed
> wire around the camp. The wire was charged with electric current.
> The camp itself was pretty decent, but a couple of rooms were
> something to see. There were two gas chambers (would take care of
> 36 in each chamber at a time). There was an elevator (just the right
> size for a body) to carry off the stiffs to the dissection room where
> there were fancy tables with nice little gutters to carry off the blood
> and a furnace to burn the remains, and a cute little room filled with
> urns in which the ashes could be sent home if the home folks kicked
> through, and a couple of piles outside where they could be thrown if
> the home folks didn't. There were also some rooms with hooks
> where people who didn't talk could be tied up, and a big pile of
> shoes and hair, of some who had previously enjoyed to a high de-
> gree the efficiency of nazi culture. A little visit to this place would
> not be amiss for each of our delegates to the Peace Conference. . . .

Finally, just days before the German surrender, American forces reached
Dachau, on the outskirts of Munich, one of the most infamous concentration camps.

> Dachau, Germany
> May 4, 1945
>
> . . . Last Sunday I went in Dachau to take over the concentration
> camp. We had our plans pretty well prepared for what we knew we
> would have to do, but it came up a little sooner and somewhat
> faster then we had planned upon. . . .
>
> The sights we saw the next few days were actually unbelievable. I
> had read many stories about the horrors of these camps, but I al-
> ways was a little bit skeptical. Now I shall believe anything for I
> know that anything is possible.
>
> As we approached the camp, one saw a horrid sight. A trainload
> of bodies. That is not entirely accurate, but nearly so. This was a
> train coming into the camp from another camp. The beasts would
> crowd these people into the cars, a hundred or more into a box car
> that was supposed to hold 40; or perhaps it was an open gondola
> car, where they were exposed to the weather, out of 4,000 people

WHi(X3)23734
Prisoners cheering the liberation of Dachau at the end of April, 1945.

transported from one camp to Dachau in the last days, only 2,000 reached it alive; and they were practically dead.

The sight of these things was almost too horrible to even try and imagine. I hate to think of it. But that was only a starter; the gas chamber, you have read about it; the place for execution by shooting, the crematory, all were horrible beyond description. And the poor souls still living. Some were the horrible sights that you can imagine. One is filled with loathing just to think of them. Living skeletons. The camp had a population of 32,000; yet the death rate for the first four months of 1945 was over 13,000.

We had quite a task for ourselves. To try and organize the camp into a going concern, reasonably respectable. Obviously you can't immediately release all the people though most of them were political prisoners. They have to be screened, checked for security purposes and dusted for lice, for there was large amounts of typhus in the camp as well as other diseases.

But we got the camp going, and you can claim the dubious honor now of having been the wife of the Commandant of the Concentration Camp at Dachau. Perhaps I sound like I am bragging a bit, but I do think we got along fine. The prisoners themselves had organized an International Committee and had set up their own self government, which organization we continued to use.

One of our greatest handicaps was the number of visitors we had. Within five hours after we had gotten started, I had at least two dozen correspondents, 2 Lt. generals, 2 major generals, 5 Brigadier generals, and a Prince showed up.

The Prince was the Prince Regent of Luxembourg, who came in at noon. I couldn't invite him to have dinner with me as all I had was cold C rations, but I told him I'd be happy to have him join me. Since all he had was K rations, we sat on the desk and shared them, plus a can of sardines I had with me. So that must have been quite a sight, seeing us there eating with our pocket knives. We had to close the door for there was still a stiff in the room across the hall, one of the guards who didn't get away, and he was getting a bit strong.

The next day we took Munich, and I had to turn over command of the camp in order to get into that city and coordinate all the Military Government functions there. That is another story though, which perhaps the next letter I write can be about.

I am going to send a couple of souvenirs of Dachau. I'll send them to Dad. One is a club they used as a persuader; the other is a piece of tanned human hide. Neither is a very pleasant memento, but neither is the recollection of that place a pleasant memory. Every American though should see the place, and perhaps had they seen it a while ago, the war would have been over much sooner. . . .

Armies of Occupation

The Allied invasion of Sicily in July and August, 1943, meant the beginning of the end for Nazi control of Europe. On June 4, 1944, Allied forces retook Rome, and Paris was liberated on August 25, to the delight of the cheering throngs. By the beginning of 1945, American, British, and other Allied forces were poised on the western border of Germany, and Soviet forces were advancing from the east. Over the next five months, the two armies would advance toward each other until they met at the Elbe River on April 25. When the Germans finally capitulated two weeks later, all of Europe became Allied-occupied territory. (Although the Allies had been dropping food to the starving populace of the Netherlands since April 10, Holland was not freed from German control until the surrender.) The task of rebuilding the Nazi destruction had begun, but people ravaged by more than five years of totalitarianism had trouble readjusting. In Italy as well, the populace faced an uncertain transition after the end of Mussolini's Fascist rule. As Charles Birt put it, "The Italians have been conditioned to leaning on some one else's shoulder for so long that now they are on there own they are bewildered and don't know just what way to jump."

Sheboygan native Tom Thomas was a twenty-eight-year-old radio announcer when he entered the army in 1941. During the first part of the war, Sergeant Thomas worked in service and supply in Morocco. After moving to Italy, however, Thomas took advantage of his background and was reassigned as a newswriter for Armed Forces Radio in Rome. Throughout the war, Thomas wrote dispatches about wartime life and sent them back to his friend Charles Broughton, editor of the *Sheboygan Press*, who published the letters. After the war, Thomas became public

American GIs and Parisians joyously took to the streets during the liberation of Paris in August, 1944. Photo: Frank Scherschel, Life Magazine, © Time Warner Inc.

relations director for the U.S. Junior Chamber of Commerce in Chicago
and then returned to school at the University of Wisconsin, where he
obtained a B.S. in pharmacy in 1949. He practiced as a pharmacist in
Sheboygan until 1971, when he retired to the Cayman Islands and wrote
occasional pieces for a newspaper there. He died in 1988.

Rome
March 1, 1945

Dear Mr. Broughton:

Seven and one half years ago I visited Rome for the first time. It
was 1937 then and Il Duce had just returned from his first meeting
in Germany with Hitler. I was at the depot along with thousands of
others to see him. Loudspeakers on every big Roman intersection
blared martial music, the crowds were animated and gay, and when
Mussolini drove from the station to his famous balcony at the Pi-
azza Venezia the street was covered with palm branches spread
before him by his admirers. Every empty wall had painted upon it
the fascist credo "Believe, Obey, Fight." Rome today is a vastly
different place.

The fascist slogans have been removed and in their stead are the
red painted "Long live Lenin", "Long live Russia", "Death to the
king", "Long live the allies". Hammer and sickle emblems are
painted everywhere. And why not? The communists are the only
group with a program and organization. Here as in North Africa
their movement is by far the most outstanding. They have the best
pictures, the best pamphlets, the most vigorous workers. Strange to
think that once the American way of a republic and a democracy
had as much revolutionary fervor and as many international zealots
as the communists today. But that was almost 175 years ago, and
today we don't feel that way about things. So cold have become the
ashes of the American Revolution that one would flirt with a chain
gang were he to publicly proclaim the political principles of Tom
Paine[8] in a place like Georgia.

Now the people of Rome are bewildered. We've taken away their
beliefs and offered them no substitutes. Our promises of material
aid have largely gone default. Wages are frozen and food prices are
high as Vesuvius. The ration is so tiny the citizens have to patronize
the black market or starve. To eat fully and satisfy a robust appetite
costs at least ten dollars a day. Eggs alone cost 28¢ apiece. In front
of the GI restaurants run by the army for soldiers visiting Rome
stand scores of Romans begging the soldiers to bring out with them

---

[8] Revolutionary-era American patriot and writer of fiery pamphlets, such as *Common
Sense*, advocating independence from Great Britain.

a piece of bread. The other night an old lady in flawless English asked me to bring her a piece. When I came out I gave her three I had been able to sneak past the door inside my shirt. She thanked me so sincerely my throat felt tight. She was a tiny little thing of 68, a professor of painting and fine arts, the wife of a Doctor of Economics who was in his mid-seventies. They were from Budapest.

To make ends meet the middle class Roman family rents a bed to a visiting soldier on a night pass for $1.50. If there are men and especially young boys in the family there is money to be made on the black market. Dozens of ten year olds with rolls of bills that would choke a horse stand outside the PX and loiter about the GI hangouts doing business. Cigarettes go for a dollar a pack, five for six bucks. Candy bars bring up to 50¢, rouge and lip sticks $2.00. It's just like Africa, only there the market was handled entirely by Arabs and Moroccan Jews. Here the entire populace takes part. Best off in a material way are the attractive girls of easy virtue. They wear the silk stockings and enjoy the good food, collecting as high as $30. from each military man. In late afternoon and early evening the sidewalk that ascends Via Tritone is like a Freudian's dream. Girls without end stroll by, usually in twos and threes. Soldiers lean against the buildings and watch the parade, whistling knowingly at the more attractive. Oran had a similar street in Algeria. It's name has carried over here — Oranore Alley. . . .

Yours sincerely,
Tom

Robert Isaksen, born in Beloit in 1924 and raised in Delavan, entered the army and was sent to England in January, 1944. He crossed into France thirteen days after D-Day, working as an ammunition bearer and squad sergeant for an 81-millimeter mortar. Isaksen had reached the rank of staff sergeant when he wrote this letter to his uncle, Leon Isaksen, a Madison lawyer. After the war, Bob Isaksen returned to school on the GI Bill, receiving a degree in commerce and later a law degree from the University of Wisconsin. He now practices law in Middleton, a suburb of Madison.

Germany
March 11, 1945

Dear Uncle Leon,

. . . The more I see of the German people the more they confuse me. It looks to me as though they play up to who ever has the most guns. The people in places that we have just occupied put out white flags and then try to treat us as friendly as possible. They bring us

WHi(X3)47082
German prisoners of war at Echternach, Luxembourg, in February, 1945.
The GI is an interpreter. Signal Corps photo.

food and coffee, help us fix up rooms to stay in and keep up a fire in
the room. One man even helped us cut an aiming stake so we could
shoot at his own people. I would have more respect for them if they
spit on us. That would at least show they thought they were in the
right. No one can ever tell me they are poor victims of Nazi propaganda. . . .

Sincerely,

Bob

Roger G. Smith was a student and musician in Madison when he was
drafted in July, 1942. The twenty-six-year-old De Pere native worked
behind the lines in supplies and equipment, rising to the rank of master

sergeant with the 45th Antiaircraft Artillery Group, 50th Antiaircraft Artillery Brigade, and serving in France and Belgium. After the war, Smith finished his degree in business at the University of Wisconsin and moved to Battle Creek, Michigan, where he worked as a musical therapist. He died in 1983. His letters are addressed to his mother, Catherine Carney Smith.

Germany
April 17, 1945

Dear Mom and All —

... There are many slave laborers here that were left behind by the Nazi Army. They are women & men — of Russian, Polish and other nationalities. We'll regard them all as Civilians until later.

The building we are staying in is one of the very few structures that is still standing around here. We had to oust a German family in order to move in. It was rough on them for sure as we just told them to get out at once and we moved in. The Frau was terrified and put on a heart rending show for us — she cried her eyes out and begged and pleaded to stay, her furniture looked like it had been moved through two or three bombings or evictions — maybe they just salvaged it from some wrecked house. They beg and we just say — "nix verstand!"[9] and they exhaust themselves and become mortified, allmost hysterical. A yank here just takes anything he wants, what's left the Russian slaves burn up or smash if the dough boys haven't allready done so. It's really a rough deal and these Krauts are getting a good belly full of their own medicine. This place has just been taken and they've done a very thorough job. It's no different anywhere else I understand.

I sure hope I never have to be an M[ilitary] P[oliceman] or some such occupational soldier but maybe I'll have to later on for a while. I'd rather be operational. The roads are full of prisoners coming by the truckload in convoys going to the rear to be processed. I wonder what must go through their heads when they see a bunch of soldiers taking a rest along the road. The Yanks just go into a house and haul out a lot of beautiful furniture and sofas etc and sit next to the road on it — I don't blame 'em much and if the lads want to rest I guess the best is none too good. ...

Love To All
Son Rog

[9] "Nichts verstehn," German for "I don't understand."

Germany
May 20, 1945
Dear Mom;
. . . My work as usual gets me around an awful lot of the time and besides that I have just finished a three day stretch of compulsory pass time in Holland. The Dutch are really in a sad way, they've got lots of money that the Nazis printed — they bought up everything the poor Hollanders had, food is very scarce and it is forbidden for them to buy in Belgium where there is apparently everything from soup to nut[s] now. Before leaving Holland the Germans blew the dykes which rendered the bulk of their productive lands useless. Children beg you for stuff on the streets and their parents will pay anything for food — there is a terrific blackmarket in that country. Eggs are worth about 57¢ each, that is one guilder and a half — in Belgium they can be had for about 20¢ each or 9 francs. Sure is a good thing that Uncle sets up his own chow line to feed the doggies over here. The Dutch are very friendly and their beds are very soft, I was invited to one home where they had a feather tick on top of an innerspring mattress waiting for me — what a deal! The house was immaculate and everything about the place was nice, the place was decorated and furnished in excellant taste. Nothing crude about any of it, rather the furniture was rich and expensive looking. They are great people, our K ration looks like a nine course meal to them and we allways share our stuff on pass. The only beer in the city of Masterich [Maastricht], Holland is at a G.I. nite club called the "Fur Lined Fox Hole", the lads really pack the place. . . .
Love
Son Rog

The Pacific

Although the U.S. did not become involved in the war in the Pacific until the attack on Pearl Harbor, fighting had been going on for ten years as the Japanese attempted to extend their influence. During the previous decade, the Japanese had attacked Manchuria, established the puppet state of Manchukuo, and invaded China. Reports of atrocities in China inflamed American public opinion against Japan, putting pressure on the U.S. government to restrict trade with the Japanese. As tensions in the Pacific escalated, the U.S. government ordered Americans in the Far East evacuated, placed restrictions on the sale of strategic materials to Japan, placed an embargo on the sale of oil, froze Japanese assets in the U.S., and closed the Panama Canal to Japanese shipping. As relations deterio-rated between Washington and Tokyo, the Japanese decided to make a preemptive strike against the American fleet. The attack on Pearl Harbor was the result.

"Down here 90% of the people have never even seen snow"

Although life in Europe and Africa certainly was different from what most Americans in the service were used to, the South Pacific represented a still more radical departure from American custom. Even training in the southern part of the United States could not prepare soldiers for life in the jungles of places like New Guinea and Luzon. The threat of Japanese air attack was constant. F. L. "Woody" Weston described his "1st baptism of strafing" by enemy planes in the Philippines: "I greeted them not with open arms — but with a very definite and real hugging of mother earth — as represented by a mud puddle by a coconut tree." Furthermore, travel around the vast Pacific Ocean often required long stretches aboard ships, which had their own set of requirements and customs.

Duane Alexander was born in New Glarus in 1918 and in 1929 moved to Madison. He was employed in the advertising department of the *Wisconsin State Journal* when he decided to enlist in the Wisconsin National Guard in January, 1941. Staff Sergeant Alexander was sent to Australia in April, 1942, as a medical administrator with the 135th Medical Regiment. He later served in New Guinea and the Philippines, where he was awarded a battlefield commission by General Douglas MacArthur in November, 1944. Alexander remained in the army until his retirement in 1962 with the rank of lieutenant colonel. He now lives in Arizona.

While serving in the war, Alexander wrote often to his former colleague and friend at the *State Journal*, Don Anderson. Because of the lack of time and energy to write letters, American servicemen would sometimes type a single letter that they would mimeograph and send to multiple correspondents, with a personalized note at the end. This letter provides an example of this practice.

New Guinea
March 1, 1943
To All My Friends and Relatives, especially Don Anderson:
    . . . It will be impossible for me to tell you all of my experiences thus far, as censorship regulations *are* a little strict. Our Regimental censorer has been known to have a bad case of "scissoritis", and consequently letters have reached home looking like a roll for a player piano. (I hope it doesn't happen here.)
    It has been very warm up here in New Guinea, but an entirely different heat than encountered in Australia. The thermometer would probably hover around the 100 mark, with a slight breeze now and then. Most of the men have elevated their tents to take every advantage of any relief. In reading some of your letters speaking of snow, ice, and zero weather make all the "Wisconsinites" of the Regiment very envious. The last snow any of us encountered

was during our Xmas leave in 1941, and that has been long ago. Down here 90% of the people have never even seen snow. . . .

The laundry problem has been quite prevalent up here, so one of the fellows from the motor pool decided to relieve himself a little bit by building a washing machine. This was accomplished by using an old gasoline barrel, a couple of wooden paddles, a one lung gasoline motor — Presto — a washing machine. He allowed me to use it the other day, and I hope he will consider me a steady customer for the duration.

We have been very fortunate since our arrival as far as entertainment is concerned. The Special Services have arranged for movies at least twice a week. These are shown in our out door theatre and

An American soldier on Midway Island hanging out his laundry, 1942. Photo: Frank Scherschel, Life Magazine, © Time Warner Inc.

Letters from the Front

the show goes on rain or shine. Many times we have sat through a show in a heavy down pour, but no one kicked too much, as it is about the only recreation available. The other night we had Abbot and Costello in "Pardon My Sarong", and last night "Ship Ahoy" with Eleanor Powell, Red Skelton. Which, by the way, was enjoyed very much. We all hope the movie industry continues to send the films over here. . . .

Sincerely,
Duane

Louis A. Schauer, from Hartford, northwest of Milwaukee, was a twenty-five-year-old employee of Milwaukee Gas Light Company in November, 1940, when he enlisted in the Army Air Corps as an aviation cadet. He was trained as a navigator and received his commission as second lieutenant at Hickam Field in Hawaii on December 6, 1941. Schauer participated in the Battle of Midway and in the bombing of Wake Island. In 1943 on a search mission out of Espiritu Santo, an island in the New Hebrides southeast of New Guinea, Schauer's plane ran out of gas and was forced to make a night landing on a coral reef near an uninhabited island controlled by the Japanese. Two days later, Schauer and his crewmates were finally picked up by a seaplane. In 1944 he returned to the United States, where he spent the remainder of the war training the crews of B-24s and B-17s in navigational skills. He was discharged from active duty to inactive duty with the rank of major in 1946 and received his final discharge in 1957. He worked for the Michigan Consolidated Gas Company in Ludington until his retirement in 1978, and he still resides in Ludington. He wrote to Lillian Otto Fried, his supervisor when he worked at Ann Emery Hall at the University of Wisconsin, from which he was graduated in 1937.

Somewhere in the South Pacific
August 8, 1943

Dear Mrs Fried,

. . . Since I last wrote to you I have taken quite a trip by boat. Excuse me it wasn't a boat it was a ship! Although I had been across the equator by plane twice before I had never been intiated as a shellback so I caught it on the ship. — The afternoon before the crossing we had to stand polliwog watch. A polliwog being what you are before the crossing. For this we were dressed as follows: sun helmet, shirt, wing collar with a shoestring bowtie, no pants, colored short garters, no socks, shoes, coco-cola bottle binoculars, and a mop. We were given specific instructions before going on watch what we should do. If the bosun came along we had to salaam three times and proclaim in a loud voice, "A mighty man the bosun and greatly to be feared." If the ship's mess officer came by we had to stand on one leg and say, "We have no food to offer." If the executive officer came by we had to present arms with the mop and proclaim in loud voice, "clean ship, isn't it!" If the chaplain came by we had to assume a pious attitude. If another polliwog passed we had to put the index finger of our left hand under our nose, raise our right hand and shout in a loud voice "Heil!" During the watch we were doused with water from many unexpected sources. About five o'clock Davy Jones and his motley crew appeared and served us all with summons to appear in King Neptune's court the next morning. The night was spent in anxious wonderment of what would be our fate on the morrow. The next morning dressed only in our shorts we were initiated two at a time. First we had to roll in salt water on the deck and get thoroughly wet. Then we had to run through a long line of paddlers up to King Neptunes throne where we had to kneel and grasp a steel rod through which they shot electricity. If we let go we got paddled from behind. Then we were passed judgement on by King Neptune and had to run another gauntlet of paddlers to a ladder leading up to a platform on which we were sat in a greased chair. They made us take a bite of soap and then put axle grease on our chest, face, and in our hair. Without warning the chair was tipped back and we slid into a large tank of water, where we were dunked many times. We ran one more gauntlet of paddlers and we were full-fledged shell-backs. There sure were some plenty red and sore fannies that night. For this we received a membership card for our wallet and a beautiful scroll suitable for framing. It really was a lot of fun though and broke the monotony of the trip. . . .

Lt. Louis A. Schauer

Harold J. Tidrow was a thirty-four-year-old printer at the *Wisconsin State Journal* when he was drafted in July, 1943. He served with the Engineers Army Service Commission in the Philippines and in New Guinea, reaching the rank of sergeant before his discharge in August, 1945. He returned to his position at the *State Journal*, where he worked until 1970. He died in 1977. Private Tidrow addressed this letter to Don Anderson.

Philippines
February 6, 1945

Dear Don:

. . . I have made quite a few Filipino friends and a couple Sundays ago was invited to one's home for dinner. We had chicken cooked 3 different ways, fish, shrimp, rice, wine called Nipa and cocoanut candy. After dinner coffee in the living room. They have a 19 yr old daughter named Rosario. I took her walking, when we returned played cards then when I was about to leave they wrapped me a roast chicken and bottle of wine to take back to camp with me. Was to another friends house the other evening, he is a chemist, has a very pretty wife, both went to college in Manila. They gave me a large filipino orange. I'm not streching it a bit, it was bigger than a grapefruit. Also showed me a rock collection of all the minerals in the P.I. — A Q[uarter] M[aster] Co put on a Filipino dance the other evening, I didn't get to go but heard they had good entertainment and could see the girls going and they were dressed very pretty. Talked to a buddie of mine who went and he said the Yanks are too tall for most of them kinda had to look down to talk to them. At first the girls didn't dance close but in about 10 min or less the Yanks had them well covered in their arms. . . .

Tidrow
PFC

"They are all heroes to the end"

Because of censorship, Americans in the military were limited in their ability to describe the Pacific war. Nonetheless, their American correspondents, without always knowing exactly where their loved ones were stationed, learned of the difficult conditions under which Americans fought.

The course of the war, which had begun badly with the surprise attack on Pearl Harbor, soon turned for the worse. In April, 1942, some 12,000 Americans and their 65,000 Filipino allies surrendered to Japanese in the Philippines. The ensuing Bataan Death March resulted in the death of 10,000 soldiers, including 2,000 Americans. A month later, the island fortress of Corregidor fell to the Japanese, and American forces (including a number of Army nurses) had no choice but to surrender.

However, strategic victories in the Battle of the Coral Sea in May, 1942, and the Battle of Midway Island in June of that year started to the turn the war in the Allies' favor, although three years of hard jungle fighting and island hopping remained. The letters of "Dag L.," Peter Pappas, and Stewart Yeo (printed below) describe conditions during the Allies' southern offensive, during which troops fought their way through the Solomon Islands and New Guinea and eventually invaded the Philippines in October, 1944. The letters of Donald Easum, Vivian Croake, and Fred Draeger provide accounts of the fighting and extensive loss of life in the campaign westward through the islands of the Central Pacific toward Japan that culminated in the fierce fighting on Iwo Jima and Okinawa in early 1945.

An unidentified writer named "Dag L." wrote to his former supervisor at Ann Emery Hall at the University of Wisconsin describing the use of motor torpedo (PT) boats. PT boats were one of the Navy's most glamorous vessels. The small, light craft had a reputation for performing amazing feats. Unfortunately, because of their diminutive size, when the enemy hit them, the damage was often devastating.

Somewhere in the South Pacific
February 8, 1943

Dear Mrs. Fried:
Received your Xmas card just a few days ago and was certainly glad to hear from you. Since our last correspondence quite a change has taken place, as you can readily guess. As to myself, am in the Navy and the M[edical] O[fficer] for the P.T. boats in our area. The work in itself is interesting at times, & also quite boring. However this is war in the true sense of the word & we of the P.T.'s perhaps realize it more than the rest of the Navy. We have met the Japs in actual combat many times (more than you would suspect), & we have really done remarkably well. For some reason the Navy is not

IMPERIAL JAPANESE ARMY

1. I am interned at Philippine Internment Camp No. 1

2. My health is — excellent; good; fair; poor.

3. Message. (Limited to 25 words.)

Anxious to know that everyone is well and how to picture all. Am keeping busy and well. Please send love to Elva and P il. Love.

Signature

WHi(X3)47101

Lieutenant Marcia Gates of Milwaukee was one of about sixty U.S. Army nurses captured by the Japanese when Corregidor fell in May, 1942, and was held until February, 1945. This postcard represents one of the few messages received by Gates's family during her captivity. After the war, Gates continued her nursing career, including service in Japan during the Korean War, until her death in 1970 at the age of fifty.

publishing the damage we are doing, but suffice to say they are satisfied (Navy headquarters). I have been most fortunate — fired on, strafed by airplanes, have had hair breath escapes, but so far God is on my side. Not so for all of us, because we have had our losses & when one of our frail boats is hit — there is no more. Out of one boat — no one saved — another one survivor & he a permanent physical wreck. It is not easy to watch your roommates get blown to Hell — but that is war. Personally, I wouldn't advise anyone to try P.T. boats regardless of what they read — most of it is so different now than when Bulckeley[10] did his bit of work — one example — he says never go after a destroyer — well, out here, destroyers & cruisers are all we get to go after. None of the boys say a word, however, & they are all heroes to the end.

My hospital is in a "native village" near the base — treat my own boys & natives as well. Have already been offered a wife by the chief of the tribe, but must say I am still single. . . .

As ever —

Dag L.

Peter G. Pappas was born in La Crosse in 1917 and attended La Crosse State Teachers College and the University of Wisconsin Law School, where he was enrolled at the start of the war. In July, 1942, he was drafted and became an intelligence and supply officer with an antiaircraft battalion, serving in the invasions of New Britain, Hollandia, Leyte, and Luzon. Captain Pappas returned to the United States in December, 1945, and received his discharge in March, 1946. He finished his law degree at the University of Wisconsin and then received a master's degree in law from Harvard University. Pappas currently is a circuit court judge, a position he has held since 1969. His letters are to his former teacher, Myrtle Trowbridge.

New Guinea
February 25, 1944

Dear Miss Trowbridge,

. . . We had our first taste of accomplishing our mission and had a great variety of experiences. Because of my acquaintance with the Intelligence officers of infantry units I spent some time at the front lines — if one can form such things in this jungle warfare. Seeing the dead, the putrid Jap corpses and the accompanying battle labors was far from pleasant but it was not the shock I expected it to be.

---

[10] Lieutenant John D. Bulkeley, commander of Motor Torpedo Boat Squadron 3, who engineered the defense of the Philippines with only a few airplanes and small PT boats for more than four months after the Japanese attack on the islands.

Further, I was surprised at the state of casualness with which much of the fighting was done. True, we didnt have the problem of Tarawa[11] but a couple of battles were equally as fierce. However, our auto aircraft mission is far different than the infantry in this theatre — and we were busy at night. We have destroyed a couple planes and have succeeded admirably in keeping bombers out of this area. To see a full-fledged ack-ack[12] barrage at night is better than five acts of Vaudville — and there is an impersonal delight in seeing a direct hit cause a Jap bomber to disintegrate in the sky.

Many a night we spent hours in our trenches — and, if the raid was a surprise we usually had time to grab only a helmet while in mid-air from cot to fox-hole.

The first couple weeks were rough; wet clothes; no shelter; excessive rain and mud; dirty clothes; cold rations. Several nights my jungle hammock only served to collect rain so by morning I'd be sleeping in a couple inches of water. When morning came I merely took my clothes off; squeezed the excess water out and put them on for another day. If I had been able to remove my shoes there was usually a quart of water in each of my small boots to be poured out. Yet, it had its humorous aspect when I recalled former days of luxury at home and school.

Despite our finding it rough; we had a picnic as compared to the infantry — they really get the dirty work. I'll take my hat off to them anyday; they are the real soldiers. Nights in shallow trenches half full of water; even cold rations irregularly and no chance to remove clothes for a dip in a stream plus the nervous tension of this hidden warfare. All of our branches are coordinated for terrific blasting force at last but the "G-men of Battle" has to actually clear the enemy and occupy the territory in dispute. . . .

Following his service in Hawaii (see pp. 75–76), Stewart C. Yeo moved on to New Guinea in 1943, to Morotai in 1944–1945, and to the Philippines in 1945–1946, serving as a field artillery officer. After service in the Korean War, Yeo retired from the army in 1956 and went into the real estate business. He died in 1988.

Morotai
October 29, 1944

Dear Dad:

No doubt you have read about the strike on Leyte by the South

[11] Tarawa was a tiny coral atoll in the Gilbert Islands where four days' bitter fighting in November, 1943, cost the U.S. Marines 991 killed and more than 2,300 wounded.
[12] Anti-aircraft.

West Pacific forces and also about the recent naval battle there.[13] The Japs see the handwriting on the wall and realize it's just a matter of how long before we start setting up our tents in Tokio. Obviously it will take some time because in this theatre even if we had *slight* opposition from one base to another this amphibious war takes time. It's not like being on the continent of Europe. Even though the Japs are being weakened as we grow stronger they still have more forces to oppose us as we approach Japan and we will have to do more to help China then we have so far. The guerilla forces in the P[hilippine] I[slands] have been very active and are much larger than people imagined. We have detailed and accurate information of the Philippine situation especially Luzon and it's largest city Manila. We know for instance from day to day just which units are in which buildings in Manila. We know there is a 105mm Jap gun under a tree at the cross roads just 1 kilometer south of a certain village; so thorough is our intelligence. We have numerous agents there and as you know the Philippinos are natural born guerillas. Witness the insurrection we had to put down and it lasted several years after '98 in the Southern Islands. Have been reading numerous reports of Jap prisoners of war who have been in Manila and Luzon in general. Many places are mentioned which are familiar to me. They are trying to woo the natives of the P.I. to their "Greater East Asia Prosperity Sphere" but the natives don't understand the Jap paying them little or nothing for goods, and their broken promises. It serves to show the Philippinos that Uncle Sam was very magnanimous and even overlooked their lack of appreciation for what we did for them up to the war. We have settled down to routine here now. We have just about completed our mission which was the construction of air fields for use against forward opposition. We still have daily Jap air raids but our anti-air craft protection is so tight now that they seldom drop any bombs where it counts. Our doughboys on the perimeter are killing off the remnants and driving the nips into the mountainous jungles. We all hope we can move on soon.

Best Regards
Stewart

Some of the hardest fighting of the war took place in early 1945 during the campaign through the islands of the western Pacific. From February 9 to March 11, fierce fighting ensued on Iwo Jima, an eight-square-mile

[13] On October 20, 1944, Allied forces invaded Leyte, an island in the Philippines. From October 24 to 26 the largest naval engagement in history took place in Leyte Gulf and off the coast of Samar. When it ended, most of the remaining Japanese fleet had been destroyed.

island in the Nanpo Shoto, a chain of islands extending 750 miles south from central Japan. When the battle ended, 6,821 Americans had died and another 18,070 had suffered injuries. On April 1, Americans moved on to Okinawa, in the Ryukyus, islands only 360 miles from the home islands. By June 21, when organized resistance on Okinawa ended, more than 12,000 Americans had been killed and another 36,800 had been injured, many of them by kamikaze or suicide attacks on U.S. ships off Okinawa. The following two letters — the first composed during the battle of Iwo Jima by Corporal Donald B. Easum and the second written in the battle's aftermath by hospital recreation worker Vivian Croake — describe the battle and its effects.

Donald B. Easum was born in Culver, Indiana, in 1923, and moved to Madison at the age of seven, when his father, Chester, became a professor in the University of Wisconsin's history department. After graduation from high school, Donald enrolled at the university but left in March, 1943, to join the army's Enlisted Reserve Corps. Easum, a corporal with the 147th Army Airwaves Communications Service, served in Hawaii and

American soldiers landing in Dutch New Guinea, 1944. WHi(X3)14583

at Iwo Jima. After the war, Easum finished his B.A. in history at the U.W. and later received an M.A. and Ph.D. from Princeton University. In 1953 Easum entered the U.S. Foreign Service, with postings in Nicaragua, Senegal, and Niger before becoming ambassador to Upper Volta (1971–1973) and Nigeria (1975–1979). Easum was also U.S. assistant secretary of state for Africa in 1974–1975 and was a member of the National Security Council. After his retirement from the Foreign Service in 1979, he served as the president of the African-American Institute in New York City until 1988.

At the time of the Iwo Jima landing, Easum was one of the "specialized garrison troops" who landed soon after the invasion to help operate the first airstrip seized by the Marines. He mailed this letter to his parents when censorship restrictions were lifted after the Japanese surrender.

Iwo Jima
February 21, 1945

Since early morning of Feb. 19 we have been in sight of Iwo Jima island, awaiting debarkation orders. At 0900 of that day, Marines landed on the southeast beach. For two days previous, battleships and cruisers bombarded the island, and they are still doing so in coordination with TBF Avenger dive bombers and F4F Wildcat fighters modified to carry rockets slung and fired from beneath the wings.

Even before any landings were attempted, Radio Tokio reported two such had been repulsed. The facts were further distorted when the same source claimed, two days ago, that Japanese fighter interceptors had shot down more than thirty American planes. In reality, the seventy-one consecutive days of bombing by Saipan based B-24's and B-29's from Saipan and the new double runway on Tinian, plus the concentrated pre-invasion naval bombardment, so saturated the tiny fortress island some 700 miles from Tokio that not a single Jap plane has been airborne. On D-Day, from our transport, two carrier-based planes were seen to crash into the sea, presumably victims of the then sporadic, now silent, anti-aircraft. The 300 landing boats claimed by Tokio to have been sunk are still landing men and supplies on the beachhead.

But the conquest of Iwo Jima will not be easy. The first few invading waves encountered slight initial resistance, but on the level plateau above the beach where protecting cover was slight, machine gun fire was concentrated and deadly. Mortars and artillery entrenched in caves on the rocky volcanic promontory at the lower end of the island rained explosives on the beachhead. Small landing boats from our transport were used to land medics and evacuate casualties. Their crews, hurriedly devouring sandwiches and oranges in our galley, told of bodies piled like cordwood on the beach. A man with BONARD, A. G., stenciled on his jacket, related, with a trace of a French accent, how he had piloted his little boat back and forth from beach to hospital ship, each time passing literally beneath the 16 inch guns of a battleship pulled in close to blast away at the volcanic mountain arsenal. "Tanks, jeeps, boats — their wreckage smeared all over the beach — what a mess," he said quietly; "but those Marines! — by Jove, I hand it to them — calm and cool — and the weight they carry on their backs is more than I could lift. Two holes in my boat — mortar fire hit all around us." How could he be French and say "by Jove?"

By official reports, our beachhead is now 5000 yards long and 500 yards deep. But it has also been reported that we hold one airfield, presumably the southern one. This would indicate the penetration approximates a mile and a half at least at one point.

Naval encirclement of the island could be roughly divided into three categories. The inner circle consists of battleships and cruisers — it surrounds the island, pounding obstinate gun emplacements. Within this circle, just off the southeast beach, LCI's, LCM's, LCT's,[14] and assault boats and smaller craft of all sorts. The outer circle is a perimeter of defense having a circumference of several hundred miles, and consisting largely of destroyers and carriers. Between these two loops of steel, one offense, one defense, lies a huge armada of transports waiting orders to land their cargo of specialized garrison troops and equipment. The majority of these lie off the southeast coast of the ten-square-mile island.

Yesterday a cruiser came up alongside to receive shells and powder, but the sea was so rough she damaged our hull. She drew off, and the explosives were transferred by small boats.

At night bouquets of orange fire-flowers, trailing billows of white cottony smoke, indicate the use of phosphorus shells on the island. The majority of them have been seen to be fired from the north end of the island toward the center, while from the center against the north end are clearly visible the liquid red spurts of flame throwers.

As yet there has been only one landing. If resistance remains as stubborn as it is now, I anticipate a second, perhaps on the opposite, west beach. If our strategy was to cut the island in half, and then advance against the ends, it has failed, so far.

---

[14] "Landing Craft Infantry," "Landing Craft, Mechanized," and "Landing Craft Tank." Unlike older types of ships, which required smaller boats to ferry cargo ashore, these new large transport ships could sail close to land and discharge their cargo down ramps into shallow water.

The Army-Navy-Marine cemetery on Guam, which was retaken in July, 1944. From the Dickey Chapelle collection, State Historical Society of Wisconsin.

Profiting no doubt by experience gained in Luzon landings, all floating objects near our ship are fired upon by men armed with sub-machine guns. However, to my knowledge there have as yet been no Japanese submarine activities, much less human torpedo attempts.[15] No enemy aircraft have been sighted. Our naval aircraft are ubiquitous, flying both in formation and single above and around the island, and in patrol over the surrounding seas.

Vivian Croake was serving as a hospital recreation worker in Hawaii (see pp. 82-84) when she wrote to her former boss, Leon E. Isaksen, describing battle casualties.

Hawaii
June 25, 1945

Dear Mr. Isaksen,

. . . I wish I could tell you more stories about my work — the bravery and courage of young fellows with both eyes gone — or limbs or arms. The worst was after Iwo. I shall never forget that as long as I live. Most of the casualties were in pretty good spirits as their first reaction was that they were lucky to even be alive after seeing so many slaughtered. The hard part for them will be in the years to come when Iwo will just be a name. It has been most difficult to keep emotionally detached. I was extremely interested in reading the other day that the number of flyers lives saved because of emergency landings on Iwo so far, just about equalled the number of Marine lives lost.

I am dealing quite a bit with psychiatric patients now, and to me they seem more pathetic than physical disability cases. The tragedy of many of the cases is that they have been brought about by the cruelty of our own men. Not intentionally of course but by lack of understanding. . . .

Sincerely Yours,
Vivian

After his training (see pp. 79–80), Fred J. Draeger was stationed on the U.S.S. *Bunker Hill*, an aircraft carrier, as an aviation ordnanceman first class. In 1943 and 1944, the *Bunker Hill* participated in numerous operations in the South and Central Pacific before returning to Bremerton, Washington, in November, 1944, for repairs to damage suffered five months earlier during the Battle of the Philippine Sea. In January, 1945, the *Bunker Hill* returned to the Western Pacific, where the ship provided

[15] Between December, 1944, and January, 1945, around the island of Luzon (on which Manila is located), Japanese kamikaze raids sank a total of twenty-four ships and damaged sixty-seven others, causing shipboard casualties of 1,230 dead and 1,800 wounded.

WHi(X3)47079

Servicemen on board an aircraft carrier exercising among their planes. Official U.S. Navy photo. From the Philip La Follette collection.

support for raids by the 5th Fleet on Japan and the Ryukyus from February 15 to March 4. The *Bunker Hill* also supported the fighting at Iwo Jima and Okinawa. On May 11, 1945, during the latter encounter, the ship was hit by two kamikaze planes and suffered serious damage, including nearly 400 dead and more than 250 wounded. Draeger wrote to Joseph Helfert, editor of the *Beaver Dam Daily Citizen.*

Somewhere at Sea in the South Pacific
April 25, 1945

Dear Joe:

. . . Well Joe, censorship now permits me to mention some of the operations we've taken part in since leaving the U.S. (that is up to Mar. 1st). The first and probably most spectacular was the original "set-to" on Tokyo and surrounding areas, Feb. 16–17. That surprised a lot of people, including the Japs. I was most astonished at the weather and rough seas encountered (a bit chilling for my equatorial plasma). You've got to hand it to our boys flying through

sleet, snow, and rain and back again to a bobbing runway of doubt-
ful stability. And did they lay the eggs into vital targets — The ele-
vation of the "Rising Sun" was held to a minimum those days as
our boys were on them like hawks bagging them left & right. We
also were on the coverage & invasion of "Iwo Jima" Feb 19–21–22.
The Japs took a terrific beating there in spite of their natural defense advantages — It must have shaken the smart boys back in
Tokyo to know our forces would not be stopped. They thought Iwo
an unsurpassable front porch, but she's gone now, steps and all. —
We rapped at the front door again when Tokyo took another beating Feb 24–25. On Mar. 1st we were in on the Okinawa strikes
(Ryukyu's). Well that's as far as I'm allowed to go for the time being. Our fighters do a bang up job knocking 'em off on the outskirts
all through the operations — If some of the Nips do get through our
ships gunners blast them with arsenals of flack. There are some
close one's but you can bet we hold a mighty big edge on them. . . .

as always
— Freddy

"Do you know what it feels like to make a bombing run?"

For those in the air, the war was a very different experience than for
ground troops. Fighter pilots in particular had a kind of glamour about
them that foot soldiers lacked. One of the latter, Harold J. Tidrow, wrote
in November, 1944, that "Major Bong from Popular [sic] Wis is here
close to us and I seen him knock down a Jap bomber," referring to ace
pilot Richard Bong in much the same way that other soldiers referred to
movie and sports stars.

A. Roger Conant grew up in Marinette, on Green Bay, and attended
the University of Wisconsin. He entered the navy in 1941, during his
senior year of college, when he joined a flight training program in
Glenview, Illinois, with a unit called the "Flying Badgers" that included
others from the university. Conant served overseas as a F4U Corsair
fighter pilot from January, 1943, to April, 1944, stationed primarily in the
Solomon Islands and on Midway Island. He flew approximately 100
combat missions and shot down six Japanese fighter planes. Conant returned to the United States and was on his way back to the Pacific as a
night fighter pilot when the war ended. He received his discharge in
October, 1945, but stayed in the reserves until 1956, in which capacity he
was recalled for two years of active duty in the Korean War. Conant flew
commercial airliners and then joined Douglas Aircraft as a test pilot in
1952. He now lives in Newport Beach, California. He wrote to Lillian
Otto Fried and the other staff members at Ann Emery Hall, where he had
worked as a waiter while at the U.W.

Midway Island
May 13, 1943
Dear Ann Emery Mob:
I've wanted to write you for a long time, but it's not an easy job here. We have only one table, so I have to wait my turn. Then too, there's very little to write, because I do the same thing every day and that's censored. I guess it's O.K. to tell you I'm [*censored*] in the South Pacific. That's not too hard to guess anyway. Also, I'm a fighter pilot. That may be censored, but I doubt it. It's not such a thrilling life. In fact, quite the contrary. I've never really been quite so bored as I am now. Funny thing tho. I remember back at Ann Emery, we used to argue about the things that were impossible to do in an airplane. Now I do those things every day & it's boreing. Never thought I'd see the day! . . .

Today I painted the name on *my* plane. "The Dragon Lady". Do you like it? The mode of our squadron tends toward the Pirate an-

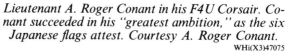

Lieutenant A. Roger Conant in his F4U Corsair. Conant succeeded in his "greatest ambition," as the six Japanese flags attest. Courtesy A. Roger Conant.
WHi(X3)47075

gle. Most planes have names like Capt. Kidd, Henry Morgan, etc. I had several names but they were all taken before me. I get the Dragon Lady from "Terry and the Pirates"[16] and tho she may not really be a pirate it's a good name. My crew and I are sure proud of that plane. Our greatest ambition is t[o] add Jap flags under the cockpit. We'll do it, too, as soon as they start doing a bit of fighting in this ocean. Damn Africa!

Give my regards to all, Sincerely

Roger

After Dick Bong finished his training, he joined the 5th Air Force as a second lieutenant in September, 1942, and served in New Guinea, where he was promoted to captain. In April, 1944, he broke Eddie Rickenbacker's World War I record of twenty-six enemy kills, a feat that earned him a promotion to the rank of major and a case of scotch from Rickenbacker. In October, 1944, Bong moved with his squadron to the Philippines, where he flew missions until December, when he was awarded the Congressional Medal of Honor by General Douglas MacArthur.

When Bong reached forty kills in late 1944, the highest of any U.S. pilot in the war, the air force decided to return him stateside and give him a position as a test pilot. On August 6, 1945 (the same day the atomic bomb was dropped on Hiroshima), Bong died in southern California when his experimental jet aircraft crashed shortly after takeoff.

New Guinea
December 30, 1942

Dear Mom,

Well I've done it at last. Saw the Nips at close range and shot down two airplanes on Dec 27th. If you watch the news papers and Life and Time magazine you might read about it. We were congratulated by General Kinny and General Wurtsmith.[17] General Kinny is the one who grounded me in Frisco, remember?[18] I don't know if all this will go through the censor or not. Don't know if it is O.K. to

---

[16] Drawn by Milton Caniff from 1931 to 1947, "Terry and the Pirates" was a popular adventure comic strip set in China. Terry began as a young boy, but by the time of the Japanese invasion of China in 1938 he had matured enough to join the Chinese resistance fighters and later the American air force. The Dragon Lady was one of the main characters, embodying the stereotype of the mysterious oriental princess.

[17] General Paul B. Wurtsmith of the 13th Air Force.

[18] General George C. Kenney claimed that in June, 1942, while Bong was training in San Francisco, he had taken a P-38 fighter plane and done loop-the-loops around the center span of the Golden Gate Bridge and had then flown down Market Street waving to workers in the office buildings lining the route. According to Kenney's version of the incident, instead of court-martialing Bong, the general sentenced him to perform household chores for a woman who had complained that his flight had blown her laundry off the clothesline. In 1944, however, Bong claimed that he had merely buzzed the house of a friend of his, upsetting the friend's neighbors. Whatever the extent of his misbehavior, Bong was grounded for six weeks and dropped from the 49th Fighter Squadron as punishment.

WHi(X3)47078
Major Richard I. Bong receives the Congressional Medal of Honor from General Douglas MacArthur on December 12, 1944. Signal Corps photo. From the Philip La Follette collection.

say it or not but I'll hear about it if it isn't. Shot down two of them in my first encounter and got one bullet hole in my plane. Not bad at all I would say. . . .

Had an American candy bar the other day and it sure tasted good. Drank a scotch and soda on the night after my victory to celebrate. You'll probably read or have read rather in the paper where we shot down 19 airplanes in one day and that is the day I had my fun. . . .

Love,
Dick

Thurman Fox was a student at Oshkosh State Teachers College when he joined the Army Air Forces in May, 1943. He became a bombardier with the rank of second lieutenant, serving with the 13th Air Force, primarily on Morotai. After his discharge in January, 1946, Fox finished his education in Oshkosh and then became a teacher in Beaver Dam and Madison before joining the staff of the State Historical Society. In 1984, Fox retired as director of the society's museum. He described a bombing mission in a B-24 to his parents, Orville W. and Frances Fox, and his grandfather, George Smith.

Morotai

March 22, 1945

Dear Mom, Dad, & Grandad.

. . . Do you know what it feels like to make a bombing run over here. I imagine it must be the same feeling a man must have when he is riding a landing barge, but I lack that fear he must have because death rides closer to him than it does me. But going on. When you get near the target area you start looking for it, you are fairly calm, and you know what is going on then some one sees it, & shouts there it is 20° left, your heart comes in your mouth, you fall on your knees & start looking through the window for the target, you see it, you check your alt, & air speed, check your sight to see if it is set properly. The Pilot turns on the target, you are now within straffing distance, the nose gun starts firing, the noise & smoke is terrific, you start killing your course, with things running through your mind, are the racks in select, are the doors open, are the rack switches on, is the trigger on, why don't this plane turn faster, isn't the c-1[19] set up properly, your breath comes in short pants, there is a knot in the pit of you stumich, you shake all over from the excitment, and then BOMBS AWAY, you start cutting switches, tell the pilot OK to turn, you close the doors & try to observe the impacts all at the same time. You live a 1000 lives in 40 secs & then it is all over & you are on your way home, tired by your nervousness, & a calm starts settling over you, & you feel at peace with the world. You have the same experience every time. I have had six such experiences.

Guess that is all for now

From your loving son

Thurm

[19] A calculator used by both navigators and bombardiers.

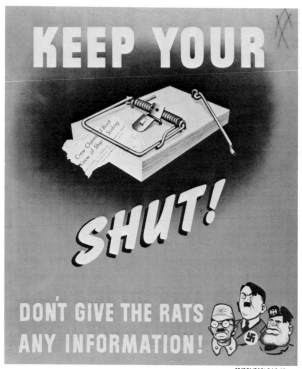

WHi(X3)31949

Some of the most striking examples of American propaganda were posters that exhorted the public to contribute to the war effort. Many such posters warned Americans to avoid revealing information that might help the enemy.

Another aspect of the Pacific war that differed greatly from that in the European theater was the attitude of American combatants toward their enemies. Whereas Carl Schluter called fighting the Germans "a 'Gentlemans' war here, you shoot first than I'll shoot," the Japanese were viewed as savages, inhumane to American prisoners (a reputation enhanced when news of the Bataan Death March was released to the public in early 1944), and filled with an almost supernatural fanaticism, as evidenced by their kamikaze missions. Stewart Yeo wrote that "Due to Jap psychology they do not surrender. In Europe the German soldier has common sense enough to know that if his situation is hopeless he might live to a ripe old age by surrendering." Few Japanese soldiers were taken prisoner, and approximately one-third of all Americans captured by the Japanese did not survive their imprisonment.

The Japanese often used radio broadcasts, which could be heard from Alaska to China (see John Koetting's letter, pp. 136–137), to purvey misinformation to American forces about the course of the war. The most famous of these propagandists was Tokyo Rose, who aired "news" aimed at lowering American morale and supposedly secret intelligence (often gathered from commonplace sources like newspapers) about American troop movements. Japanese prisoners of war also relayed information they had received from their commanders, providing a glimpse of propaganda used by the Japanese army on its own people.

In their letters, John D. "Pink" Rice, Leo Pietrucha, and Stewart Yeo provide insight into the American soldier's view of Japan. Rice, a twenty-five-year-old native of Sparta, was working for the *Wisconsin State Journal* when he was drafted in the spring of 1942. He served as a second lieutenant with Battery G of the 75th Coast Artillery, working with anti-aircraft weapons in Alaska. He was discharged in the fall of 1945 and resumed his media career, first with the *Monroe County Democrat* and later in radio, eventually owning the Sparta-Tomah Broadcasting Company, which ran stations throughout Wisconsin. In 1966 Rice ran for Congress as a Democrat but lost to former Republican Governor Vernon Thomson. Rice died in 1991. He wrote to Don Anderson.

Pietrucha was a Beaver Dam resident born in 1914 who was working for the *Beaver Dam Daily Citizen* when he was drafted in 1943. He became an infantryman and cook with the 1st Company, 19th Infantry Regiment, serving in New Guinea and the Philippines. He was discharged from the army in February, 1946, and returned to Beaver Dam, where he worked at the Monarch Range Company, a producer of kitchen appliances. Pietrucha died in 1982. He wrote to Joseph Helfert, editor of the Beaver Dam newspaper.

Alaska
March 26, 1943

Dear Don,

. . . We hear the Japs get out their daily propaganda bulletins from Tokyo on our short wave sets. The Japs have the corniest radio programs on this entire planet. Their music sounds like something out of Wagner played on a cowboy's harmonica. When our air force blew hell out of that 22-ship Jap convoy down in the south Pacific[20] the Japs didn't mention either their army or navy for a couple of weeks. Then they finally got to a point where thay admitted they had lost one ship. Yesterday they seemed to be unable to face their consciences by saying anything about their military successes and Our (always) reverses. Instead they devoted their time to "a news commentary on Gold as a Bone of Contention between Britain and the United States." There was supposed to have been a big conference, the Japs said, between financial notables. Their yarn was that the allied powers wanted to set up an international bank for financial control of the postwar world. But, the broadcast con-

[20] Probably a reference to the events of January 6–10, 1943, when the U.S. 5th Air Force attacked a Japanese convoy of ten ships heading from Gasmata, on New Britain, to Lae, on New Guinea. The Americans sank two enemy ships, damaged several more, and destroyed approximately eighty airplanes.

tinued, the whole deal fell through because the Americans wanted to have controlling interest in the institutions and the British wouldn't agree. They completely neglected to point out where the hell gold came into the matter if it had been true in the first place. Then they dragged out a yarn about their giving up their extraterritorial rights in conquered China. Although of course everybody knows that if they gave up anything at all they gave it up to their own puppet rulers. In addition they quoted a couple of prisoners, one allegedly taken in the Philippines and another in the Burma campaign. These messages from the prisoners were to the effect that all the conquered (and I presume unconquered) countries had only to "cooperate" with Japan in order [to] restore sweetness and light to this placid planet. They're all strictly from hunger.

Regards,

pink rice

Somewhere in the South Pacific

July 28, 1944

Dear Joe

Dropping you a few lines to let you know I'm still in the hospital some w[h]ere in the South West Pacific. I'm still waiting to be operated on for I have a bad jungle rash and its awful hard to get rid of. You know Joe out here in the jungles a man can get most anything and what I mean a man has to be plenty tough out here. Some of these Japs are big men, they are 6 ft. 200 lbs. boys but still the Yanks are better fighters all the way around. Some of the Japs we captured in New Guinea told us they was fighting in California and they also said that they had Chicago, New York and that it wouldn't be long & they would have us wiped out. So you can imagine what a snow job Tojo[21] is giving his people. Did you receive the Jap money I sent you for I sure hope you did. When I come back I will show you some real Jap money and a few other things that I have. Joe if you was out here you could write a story book how the natives live and what the Japs done to them. I would like to write you about a lot of things but we can not write every thing that a man seen out here.

---

[21] General Tojo Hideki, Japanese prime minister.

Well Joe I will close for this time and hoping you are in the best of health and also the rest of the family.

Your Friend Leo

New Guinea
July 15, 1944

Dear Dad:

There is a lull in activities so can write a few lines. This morning the Ordnance hauled 2 Jap field pieces up here that were captured in a fight a few days ago. They had some deep shell fragment nicks in them from our artillery fire which rendered them useless. There were also a number of light and heavy machine guns captured. Our artillery has been right up behind the infantry, supporting. The batteries have been under attack at their positions and wire and observation parties have been attacked and sniped at. The Jap is desperate — as he is everywhere in New Guinea now. He is without reserve food and ammunition supplies and he either fights to try and cut his way thru to other Jap forces or he dies for the emperor, which he doesn't mind doing. We have taken very few prisoners. When we take an artilleryman we give the intelligence officer a list of questions we are interested in about enemy artillery activities. Jap prisoners talk freely and we believe pretty truthfully. The reason for this is that the Jap code is to be victorious or die. To surrender is not in their makeup or to be captured alive; therefore the Jap officers can not tell them what to tell in case of capture, as it would infer that capture were possible for the son of heaven. Regardless of this fact many Japs do get down on their knees and surrender — more often the service troops — The well disciplined combat troops seldom surrender, if ever. We have Jap (loyal) interpreters and it is interesting to see how they work, questioning prisoners. They first feed them and give them a cigarette and get good information usually. Am enclosing a Jap calling card which in itself is nothing, but it was removed from a dead Jap on our front a couple of days ago. . . .

Best Regards
Stewart

"But don't send I to the CBI": China/Burma/India

The smallest and most remote theater of World War II was the CBI, with fewer than 200,000 Americans stationed there. In contrast to the Pacific, where American forces fought almost alone against the Japanese, the CBI theater included British, French, and Dutch troops, as well as Chinese

forces, which had been at war since 1937. Following the Japanese conquest of Burma in April, 1942, Allied forces stationed in India airlifted
goods to the Chinese resistance over the "Hump" (the Himalaya Mountains). At the end of 1943, the Allies launched a campaign to reopen the
Ledo Road, a route running from Ledo, in the Indian province of Assam,
through Burma into southern China. By spring 1945, British forces had
taken the road and rail networks of Burma. Before a coordinated effort to
begin the liberation of China could begin, the Japanese surrendered, and
the war ended.

Because the CBI theater received so little attention relative to the other
areas of the war, Signe Skott Cooper, a nurse serving with the 20th
General Hospital in Assam, India, recalled feeling as if "nobody knew
where we were and nobody cared. . . . Everybody felt like the CBI was
the end of the earth." She recalled hearing a song sung by Americans in
Europe about wanting to go home; one of the song's lines was "But don't
send I to the CBI."

Milwaukee native John Koetting was a twenty-seven-year-old student
at La Crosse State Teachers College when he was drafted in 1941. He
sailed to Australia in December, 1941, on the first troopship to sail after
war was declared and later served in both India and China as a staff
sergeant with the 51st Fighter Group. He worked in transportation and
communications and in personnel. After his discharge in September, 1945,
he finished his degree and became a teacher and assistant principal in
Arcadia, near the Mississippi River. While in the CBI, he wrote to his
former teacher, Myrtle Trowbridge.

China
May 28, 1944

Dear Miss Trowbridge,

. . . We have an advantage(?) not within your opportunities. We
hear two sides of the news. As I write Radio Tokyo is letting us in
on the know. In flawless English they relate the days events and
analyze their significance, comment on our political system, our allies, & anything else they feel is good copy. The nice thing about Jap
stations is their fine library of American records. They play the very
best in dance records for us, but not enough of them.

For the last 8 months I've had rice and pork twice a day, I feel
I'm a connoisseur of these items. I've eaten them in all shapes and
styles and I'm ready for a little change. . . .

The paddys and their accompanying water make a lot of mos-
quitoes. For the last two and a half years I've been sleeping under a
mosquito net. (Ever been under one?) They cause a little extra
bother, but they keep the insects from using the Yanks for chow,
and more, the few feet of air they encompass is the only private spot
a soldier has in China.

Experiences bring changes. I sweat bombers when they are coming and keep sweating them until they're gone, but I sweat the little
Zeroes[22] just a little more. I met an English lad in India who got run
out of Burma who said the same thing to me. At the time I couldn't
see it, but I know what he means now. I'm not alone for others in
the squadron feel the same. . . .
We see movies about 3 times a month, if some of those we see are
representative of what they show at home, I wonder how the houses
keep their customers. There are more movies in the theater, but for
reasons they don't send them all here.
I heard a rumor that houseboys may be done away with. Oh!
horror of horrors! I'll have to make my bed & shine my shoes, and
our room? who will sweep the floor and empty the ash trays?
Speaking of houseboys, I still get a kick out of this: We tell them
when we want to get up and they come in and wake us. It's almost a
pleasure. They enter soundlessly, and gently, so gently, tap us
through the mosquito netting while they whisper, "Dear Sir, it is 6
o'clock please." It usually takes them about 5 minutes to get any
results, but the method has its virtues. With this I'll close 'till another day, hoping you're well and greetings to Mr. Miller[23] and the
Faculty.

Sincerely,
John Koetting

Signe Skott Cooper, from Middleton, near Madison, was a twenty-year-
old nursing student at the University of Wisconsin when the war started.
In April, 1943, she joined the military through the Red Cross, the stan-
dard procedure at that time. Lieutenant Cooper was sent to India, where
she spent the duration of the war before moving to Burma for a month
after hostilities ended. After her discharge at the end of 1945, she returned
to Madison, where she worked at Wisconsin General Hospital (now the
University of Wisconsin Hospital) and became a professor of nursing at
the U.W. While in the army, Cooper wrote often to her mother, Clara
Skott.

Assam, India
September 26, 1944
Dear Mom,
. . . I'm working on a medical ward — officer's. The officers here
aren't quite the dope-heads they are back in the States, but it burns
me up to make beds, etc. for people when you know perfectly well if

---

[22] The Mitsubishi A6M2 Zero-sen was the best of Japan's fighter planes, and its speed,
maneuverability, and firepower exceeded that of American aircraft at the outset of the war.
[23] Leon Miller, the tennis coach at La Crosse State Teachers College.

they were enlisted men they'd be doing it themselves. Frankly, I'd just as soon work with the Chinese.

The wards are very funny. One ward has a telephone, another has a refrigerator, another the water-cooler. I practically wear out the path to the ward that has the cooler — I just can't get enough to drink. And when it's not cool, it tastes like swimming pool water. ...

The girls next door have a radio, and tonight we heard Red Skelton, and even Red Skelton sounded good.

The girls who live here are Southerners, who are used to being waited on, and all that sort of bunk, have natives to wash their clothes, etc — these women are called "ayahs", as you probably know. But none of that for me — as the guy who gave us a lecture told us "they earn extra money on the side at night" — and, anyway, there's too many bugs around here with out inviting trouble.

Nurses Signe Skott Cooper (left) and Berenice Webster making ice cream in Assam, India.
WHi(X3)47094

The Johnnies are few & far between, but today Jennie & I found one that had real Johnnie paper. The British paper we usually have reminds one of the slick pages out of Sears Roebuck catalogue! Well, I do wish I had a coca-cola — it would really be wonderful. But 2 or 3 times a week we get ice, so I put my can of grapefruit juice on ice, and it was really good.

It's raining again.

Love,
Sig

Paul Hassett grew up in Milwaukee and was living in Phelps, in Vilas County, and working as an English teacher when World War II began. Hassett, then twenty-five, enlisted in the Army Air Forces in August, 1943, and became a navigator with the 322nd Troop Carrier Squadron of the 10th Air Force. After training in Texas, Lieutenant Hassett served in Burma, flying supplies into China and dropping them to Chinese allies. He also transported Chinese and American troops into northern China to accept the surrender of Japanese troops in the region. After his discharge in February, 1946, he returned to his teaching job. He served as editor of the *Dunn County News* from 1948 to 1960, but his tenure there was interrupted when the air force recalled him to Korea in 1953. He worked in public relations for the Wisconsin Petroleum Council from 1960 to 1964, and then became executive secretary to Governor Warren Knowles from 1964 to 1970. He served as president of Wisconsin Manufacturers and Commerce from 1970 to 1986 and currently lives in Madison. His letter is to Myrtle Trowbridge.

Myitkyina, Burma
June 23, 1945

My dear Miss Trowbridge,

. . . Censorship has lifted a bit so that I can tell you where I am based. It is on the Ledo road in central Burma.

I've been flying regular combat missions with 9th squadron of 3rd Combat Cargo Group. I put in 200 combat hours, but I have just been assigned as Group Briefing Officer here. Our job is to "brief" all pilots, navigators & radio operators before they take off from here. They are only six hour shifts, but this place is a mad-house for those six hours.

The Japs do not worry us in flight; our problems are weather & rough terrain. This base is on the west side of the Hump, which is our chief flying problem now. These are the worse Jungles in the world, & with the monsoon season in full swing, flying is not much fun. I'd just as soon spend rest of my days behind the teaching desk. . . .

As my plans now stand, I expect to attend college with G.I. Bill[24] aid at least for one year after the war, and most likely for 3 years if we can arrange it financially, & I think we can. So far we been able to save a lot of money. Not sure how far it will go after the war, but with the G.I. help I think we can make it in style. I want to obtain an adequate back ground while I'm still able so I won't have too many worries in my old age.

Have a good vacation & my best wishes for your health

Paul

P.S. 1st Lt. now

Women and the War

Although most Americans who served in World War II were male, women also played a vital role in the war effort, whether working jobs at home formerly held by men, serving as nurses, working with the Red Cross, or joining the women's military services.

As a result of women's contributions to World War I, women's units were created in the early 1940s by the U.S. Army (Women's Auxiliary Army Corps, or WAAC, which later became the Women's Army Corps, WAC), Navy (Women Accepted for Volunteer Emergency Service — WAVES), and Coast Guard (SPARS, from *Semper Paratus* or "Always Ready," the Coast Guard motto). The Marines also created a women's branch but gave it no nickname. In total, 350,000 women (9,000 of them from Wisconsin) served in some branch of the military during the war.

In addition to these functions, exemplified by Vivian Croake (pp. 82–84, 125), Marcia Gates (p. 117), Signe Skott Cooper (pp. 137–139), Luida E. Sanders (pp. 141–143), Margaret Smith (pp. 143–144, 150–151), and Margaret Ebert (pp. 155–158), women also served as morale boosters for men who were lonely and far from home. Particularly in the Pacific, where many of the men lived in jungles or on barren islands, the absence of women was keenly felt and their presence was noteworthy. From the Philippines, Duane Alexander wrote that "I have never seen a Wac, Wave, Wren,[25] Spar or what have you — in person. That reminds me once again, that I have been overseas too damn long." While in the Dutch East Indies, John Marthaler wrote that "There are a few wacs about. The girls wear fatigues similar to ours so it was strictly G.I."

Despite their important contributions, women in the services were not always appreciated by their male counterparts. The attitude of many men was expressed by Richard Bong, in response to a letter telling him that his sister, Nelda, was considering joining the service, and by Louis Schauer, who heard that a friend of his at Ann Emery Hall was considering signing up.

[24] The Servicemen's Readjustment Act of 1944, which provided veterans with unemployment benefits, paid educational expenses, and offered low-interest home, farm, and small-business loans.

[25] Women's Royal Naval Service, a British women's unit.

New Guinea
April 13, 1943

Dear Mom,

. . . Nellie wrote me a letter asking me whether I thought she should join the Service in some womens organization and I wrote back and told her she was crazy if she did. I think she ought to hold a good job somewhere and build up a reserve. Most fellows in the army do not have much respect for the Waacs or such anyway. No doubt they are a good helpful organization but we just don't approve. From what I got out of her letter why she holds a pretty fair job right now and theres always room for advancement. . . .

Love,
Dick

Hawaii
June 2, 1943

Dear Mrs. Fried, Almy, and all the gang,

. . . Mrs Fried I wish you would do me a big favor. I received a letter from Marge Tallman the other day and in it she mentioned the fact that she was thinking of joining the Waves or Waacs because she didn't feel as though she was doing anything. I sat right down and wrote her that her present job was much more important than anything she would be doing in the service and it is. It is all right for someone who is waiting on table or clerking or doing some unessential office work but teaching is too important. I sure would appreciate it if you would write her and tell her to think twice before joining. . . .

Lt. Louis A. Schauer

For Luida E. Sanders, a teacher who lived in Wittenberg, in Shawano County, however, the WACs represented an attractive option. As she recalled, "As soon as I read about the women in uniform, I wanted to be ready." She enlisted in May, 1943, at the age of twenty-six and became a secretary, recruitment officer, and a hospital worker, mostly in the southern United States. After the war, she returned to school on the GI Bill, receiving a master's degree in education from the University of Wisconsin and a master's in public health from the University of California at Berkeley. She taught school in Madison, worked for the State Board of ,
Health and the Department of Public Instruction, and later obtained a real estate license. She now lives in Oshkosh. While in the army, she wrote to her mother, Ida Irene Clermont Sanders.

Fort Devens, Massachusetts
July 3, 1943

Dear Mom,

. . . We watched all the other Waacs here parade in review out on the main drill field. It was really a thrilling sight. I can't tell you how many there were (it's a military secret) but more than I had ever expected to see at one time! Next week we'll be in it, too.

We also had a formal inspection of our barracks. Last night we scrubbed on hands and knees and repacked our footlockers (trunks). This morning before 8, our beds were made, clothes hung etc. in regulation style. Then we stood at attention, looking at just one spot all the time the officers were inspecting. Our squad room was the best. There are 30 girls in it. I am again in the upper bunk in our training barracks. We have moved once already.

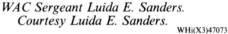

WAC Sergeant Luida E. Sanders.
Courtesy Luida E. Sanders.
WHi(X3)47073

... We got vacinated had typhoid and tetanus shots all today. Everybody looks "wilted." It hasn't affected my stomach yet but both arms are sore.

The girls go out looking for dates and call it "wolfing". Some can really do it, too. One girl makes me think of Mrs. Hull, only more so. No one likes her at all.

Tonight we're all restricted — can't leave our barracks and area because of the shots. Some girls are camped down by the road talking to soldiers.

This is a large center for training men, too. It is really a very large place. The Waac area is closed to the men, of course. . . .

The corporals are always shouting (during the day) "Fall in", or "fall out", and "on the double". We have learned to right, left and about face, count cadence, open and close ranks, and salute besides some other little things.

There is just three more weeks of basic training, then I'll probably be transferred to a regular army post. . . .

Love, Luida

De Pere native Margaret J. "Bene" Smith was twenty-seven years old and working in the family abstract business when she joined the WAVES in September, 1943. She was stationed at San Diego Naval Hospital, attaining the rank of pharmacist mate third class. On January 19, 1945, she married Harry Walker, a man she'd met in San Diego, and in May, 1945, she discovered she was pregnant, which constituted mandatory grounds for discharge from the service. On October 23, 1945, a daughter, Anne Catherine Walker, was born. The Walkers later moved to British Columbia, where Margaret was a homemaker, occasional factory worker, and administrative secretary and where she still lives. While in the WAVES, she wrote often to her mother, Catherine Carney Smith.

San Diego
May 3, 1945

Dearest Mother: —

... NOW — to tell you our very wonderful news, wonderful for us and wonderful for you too. We expect to be able to present you with a new grand-baby in November. The exact day we aren't very sure of. We'll be perfectly happy whatever it turns out to be — I'd even settle for twins but that is pretty unlikely. Just so it's healthy.

I went to see the doctor yesterday and he confirmed my suspicions without any doubt. I am overjoyed and Harry is even worse than I am about it — but personally I could do with a lot less pampering. He's always worrying that I don't get enough rest and everything else under the sun. My symptoms are nil, I've never felt better in my life. I guess I'm too disgustingly healthy.

My trip to the doctor automatically has started the ball rolling for my discharge — for all I know, it may be just a matter of days before it goes through and I will be simply Mrs. Walker, private citizen. That will be a very Frabjious day in my life I'll be able to devote my full time to what I'm really cut out for, and where my whole interest lies. I'm beyond trying to figure out whether it's right or not to have a baby during a war but war or no war it's the greatest blessing anyone could hope to have. . . .

Lots of Love
Bene and Harry

Thoughts about Home

Despite their prolonged absence, soldiers never lost interest in activities back home. In their letters, they asked about family and remembered mundane things about life at home, as Tom Thomas said in expressing his thanks for a Christmas package he received from the people of Sheboygan: "Where boys from other spots think of their towns in terms of neighborhoods or various places, we think of *all* Sheboygan and all Sheboygan thinks of us. . . . We share the same unique like of bratwurst broiling on summer nights, family picnics at Pinewoods, swimming in the lake, parking at North Point." Like Duane Alexander (p. 112–113), Wisconsin natives in the Pacific theater often mentioned how they missed snow. Those abroad also continued to follow sports, commenting on the fortunes of Badger football or their favorite baseball team.

Despite national feelings of patriotism and the desire to pull together for the war effort, things like labor unrest and political maneuvering continued, and these too interested soldiers. From April to October, 1943, the 500,000 members of the United Mine Workers union, led by John L. Lewis, went on strike in the coal mines, disregarding a "no strike" pledge made by virtually all union leaders shortly after Pearl Harbor. The federal government seized and operated the mines, brokering a settlement that resulted in an increase of $1.50 a day for each miner. As Roy F. Bergengren, Jr., complained in a letter (printed below) to Don Anderson, the miners' problems seemed trivial to those fighting the war.

In general, Americans overseas had little sympathy for home-front complaints. John F. Polchinski, from Beaver Dam, said he would like to "show some people back home what a lovely country they have to live in. Perhaps they would wake up and realize there is a War going on. . . . Some people can't seem to understand and that's what gets us fellows down." Edward C. Hoyer of Beaver Dam lambasted the "apathetical, half-hearted, and I might even say, disgraceful response the citizens of our community have made toward many of the war-effort drives." Duane Molner conveyed in his letter to a former high school teacher, Minda

Dockar, how soldiers resented those at home who were not doing their part for the war effort. Molner was a high school student in Menomonie when he enlisted in the army. He became a clerk with the 431st Signal Heavy Construction Battalion, which built and repaired telephone lines in North Africa, Sicily, Italy, and France. Molner reached the rank of technician, fourth grade, before his discharge in September, 1945. He returned to the Eau Claire area and became a business education teacher until his death in 1974 at the age of fifty-nine.

WHi(X3)47088

To cope with the enormous volume of mail sent to and from servicemen, the military developed V-mail, in which special forms were filmed and a picture of the letter was delivered to the recipient. In 1943, this drawing was sent by Corporal Stuart Koch, a former University of Wisconsin student stationed in Europe, to Lillian Otto Fried.

North Africa
July 2, 1943
Dear Don et al,
 . . . But what's all this business we read about strikes in the coal fields? Do the miners think they are among the chosen few who shall not share the suffering of this war? The lads over here and in the Pacific will expect an answer when they return. The morale of an Army whose faith is shaken in its support at home should be reason enough to bring all strikes to a halt.

We expect a few rats to profiteer in war time but we don't expect hundreds of thousands of Americans to join that class. The miners must be terribly misled but it's hard to believe they can be so stupid. And it's hard to understand why the American people allow them to get away with murder. And that's exactly what it is. Anything that slows up war production will cost the lives of American men who otherwise would live to come home. That's simple arithmetic. . . .

Apparently many Americans at home still don't realize the meaning of war, the meaning of complete sacrifice. The British know it for I've seen them. They've had war at their doorstep in the bombs that crashed down on them killing them and smashing their homes. I've seen English soldiers whose families were wiped out at home and English wives whose husbands have been gone to fight for four years. They're rationed and taxed in a way Americans have yet to dream of and complain less than the Americans. Perhaps they are to be envied for already, realizing what war means, they're preparing rich and poor alike for a better more liberal more democratic England after the war. I have nothing but admiration for them.

I hope Americans, too, will come to conceive of war and learn a lesson from it. But the mere existence of the widespread strikes doesn't paint a very pretty picture at present.

At the moment, the UMW practically represents labor to the soldier overseas. He reads about it and wonders. Are we fighting and dying so that workers may live soft lives. They don't realize it apparently but just being at home is a terrific luxury.

Picture the soldier making $60 a month. Most of this is sent home to his wife and together with a pittance from the government, makes up her monthly income. How is the rising cost of living affecting her and her children? We wonder.

I've seen that soldier in the fox holes of Tunisia. He crawled in mud or dust for 6 months. At first he was shelled by superior artillery and strafed by the Nazi airman who then ruled the skies. He

didn't know modern war — it was his first experience and sometimes he had to retreat. He saw his inexperienced friends make frontal assaults on heavily defended hills only to be mowed down. He
slept in hot sun or rain of daytime and fought in darkness over little
known territory.

But, believe me, he was heroic. He griped a little, who wouldn't?
But he never had the slightest notion of quitting. Pretty soon the
Allied planes arrived, the artillery and tanks came along, and he
picked himself up out of the mud tired and dirty, and in a trium-
phant rush he slashed the much vaunted Nazi divisions into quick
and complete submission.

Perhaps he's now in a hospital under treatment for wounds he'll
carry throughout his life. I've seen him there, too, and he's still
cheerful and he'd do it all over again.

You've had his picture and his story in the paper any number of
times. He's a hero and a great guy. His family and a few friends
actually feel every wound he received. Others admire him and perhaps work a little harder.

But what on earth can be in the heart of a man who will strike
and let this soldier down — no matter what the prevailing wage
may be, no matter what fortune some few crooks may be making.

Every man at home should see this soldier at the front, then he'd
really have an idea of what we're fighting for.

The average soldier knows he must do his job regardless of the
personal cost. He accepts the fact that he's one of the comparative
few who must risk his life to win for his country. And what more
possibly can a man give than his life? Certainly a bit of economic
hardship can't compare with that. And if it's living conditions —
I'm sure the miner's home, be it a simple shack, is preferable to a
mud hole under gunfire.

All the soldier wants of labor is a hard day's work and I'm sure
he deserves it. The striking miner surely will find little sympathy
from my soldier friend, and if labor does let him down, Johnny will
come home with a lot of anti-labor ideas which will be only the
normal reaction but which certainly won't help make that better
land after it's over.

These things are hard to put into words. You have to see them. I
didn't mean to rave so long but I promise you I have stated a uni-
versal feeling. I'm damned proud of American soldiers and hate to
see anyone hurt them needlessly. And I'm sure the American people, who after all are of the same material as their soldiers, won't

allow much more of the UMW or should I say John L Lewis monkey shines. . . .

Love and kisses,
Bergie

Italy
February 3, 1945

Dear Mrs. Dockar:

. . . Eventually the bitterness of the cold is slowly forgotten when one brings into the scene the misery and suffering of our men in a less fortunate position than what I'm in at the present. A certain amount of resentment is present over here to the many back home (there's always that minority), whose thoughts run in other channels; that is, the type who wish for a prolonged continuation of the war in order to get that mortgage paid off on their home, or the type that spends all of their time in luxurious places of amusement thus causing their absence from their vital defense job the proceeding morning and thereby causing a serious bottleneck in production of the necessary equipment which is required to successfully win many decisive battles and ultimately the ghastly war. Fortunately this is only small category and nothing will change it unless we should go through the same seemingly frightful, hectic day that our loyal ally England endured during the early stages of the war. Obviously this is not relished whatsoever, but I wouldn't be surprised to hear some day over the wireless that the Germans had successfully launched a few of their latest secret rockets at one of our east coast cities as a retaliatory measure for the inevitable collapse which is imminent in "Deutchland." . . .

Sincerely,
"Duane L. Molner"

GIs continued to follow politics while in the service. During the 1944 election, President Franklin D. Roosevelt was elected to an unprecedented fourth term, defeating Republican Thomas E. Dewey. Nearly 2.7 million Americans serving overseas (including more than 80,000 from Wisconsin) cast absentee ballots. On the election, Madisonian Howard McCaffrey commented, "I was glad to see FDR re-elected. Granted, Tom Dewey is a good man, but my fear was of the old-guard Republicans behind him, such as those who wrote his speeches." Just five months after the election, however, Roosevelt died, and a relative unknown, Vice-President Harry S. Truman, became president. This change provoked comments by Thurman Fox (writing to his parents, Orville and Frances, and his grandfather, George Smith) and Ole Oines (writing to his former teacher, Myrtle Trowbridge).

Morotai
April 13, 1945

Dear Mom, Dad, & Grandad,
Well, now what? Roosevelt is dead, where do we go from here?
Things will really be in turmoil now, won't they? About all I can say
is its better to have Truman enstead of Wallace.[26] It will be interesting now to watch the P.A.C. & Browder.[27] I'll bet the government
now takes a swing to extreme conservatism. Maybe even to
isolationism again, I hope not. I wish Bricker or Stassen[28] were in
there. . . .
A reporter is talking now on the radio in the next tent. Never
have I heard such B.S. God they talk like every soldier will commit
suicide over the death of the Commander-in-Chief. oh hum I imagine the soldier angle will be played up no end. . . .

From your loving son
Thurm

Ole Oines was born in northern Norway in 1920 but moved to Galesville,
near La Crosse, at the age of nine. He was a student at La Crosse State
Teachers College when he enlisted in 1942 and joined the Office of Strategic Services (the forerunner of the Central Intelligence Agency) overseas
in 1943. Sergeant Oines was stationed in England during the war, maintaining radio communications with people behind enemy lines on the
European continent. He was also stationed in Oslo, Norway, from May
until October, 1945, when he received his discharge. After the war he
returned to La Crosse, where he received both bachelor's and master's
degrees. He moved to Northbrook, Illinois, where he taught physics and
became treasurer of his credit union, a position he still holds.

England
April 17, 1945

DEAR MISS TROWBRIDGE:
. . . PRESIDENT TRUMAN HAS REALLY BEEN GIVEN A VERY BIG JOB
BOTH INTERNATIONALLY AND NATIONALLY. ALTHOUGH HE HAS, AS
YET, FAILED TO IMPRESS ME AS BEING THE ELOQUENT STATESMAN AND
LEADER; I AM CONFIDENT THAT OUR GREAT DEMOCRACY WILL COME
THROUGH THE COMING PERIOD NOBLY. AS YOU PERHAPS KNOW, GREAT
BRITAIN ALONG WITH ALL OF THE ALLIED NATIONS AND SEVERAL OF

[26] Henry A. Wallace, U.S. vice-president from 1941 to 1945.
[27] The Political Action Committee of the Congress of Industrial Organizations (CIO)
and Earl Browder, secretary-general of the U.S. Communist Party from 1930 to 1945.
Throughout the 1944 presidential campaign, the Republican party sought to link the PAC to
the Communists and to associate Roosevelt with both.
[28] John W. Bricker, former governor and senator from Ohio and Republican vice-presi-
dential candidate in 1944; Harold E. Stassen, former Minnesota governor and unsuccessful
candidate for the 1944 Republican presidential nomination.

THE NEUTRAL WENT INTO OFFICIAL MOURNING AT THE TRAGIC PASSING OF MR ROOSEVELT. I HEARD SEVERAL OF THE TRIBUTES THAT WERE BROADCAST, — EVEN SOME OF THOSE IN NORWEGIAN AND THEY WERE UNANIMOUS IN THEIR PRAISE FOR OUR LATE PRESIDENT. "HUMANITY HAS LOST ONE OF IT'S GREATEST LEADERS" WAS THE GENERAL TONE OF THE TRIBUTES. OF COURSE, HITLER MADE MENTION OF "THE DEATH OF THE WORLD'S WORST WAR LEADER" WOULD BE THE TURNING POINT IN THE SUCCESS OF THE NEW ORDER. . . .

MOST SINCERELY,

OLE

Another popular and controversial figure during this era was Eleanor Roosevelt, who redefined the position of first lady, taking an active role in the events of the day. At times, she was subject to harsh criticism, as is evidenced by a letter from Margaret J. "Bene" Smith to her mother, Catherine Carney Smith.

San Diego
July 17, 1944

Dearest Mother: —

. . . Eleanor Roosevelt and Admiral Ross T. McIntyre were here today — Eleanor's visit the most evident. She was to speak in the Main Patio & all ambulatory patients had to go there along with all staff members who possibly could — the patients had to tho whether they liked it or not. I didn't bother going but a lot of our Doctors did & got behind on their appointments. She kept all of them waiting three hrs. — Most of the morning in the hot sun while she breakfasted herself at Officer's Mess. Supposedly her purpose in coming was as a moral[e] builder for the patients and succeeded in only embarrassment for herself. The biggest part of her audience consisted of Marine Casualties from the South Pacific & all were without enthusiasm. You see they haven't forgotten her crack she made about Marines after she toured the South Pacific last year she said that Marines who've seen S.P. duty & fighting shouldn't be allowed to come back here as they weren't socially or morally fit to associate with American Citizens & should be left on islands.[29] I don't imagine the families of Marines who ever heard about it would show her much hand clapping or cheering either — first lady or not.

[29] In the fall of 1943, Eleanor Roosevelt toured the Pacific, stopping on seventeen islands and covering 23,000 miles by air. Despite a search of contemporary press accounts and the secondary literature, the editors could not locate the statement attributed to Mrs. Roosevelt in the letter.

Margaret J. "Bene" Smith of the WAVES enjoys a night out and drinks with two friends on the naval base in San Diego. Courtesy Dora Mae Smith.

Why in hell doesn't she settle herself down & join a nice quiet old lady sewing circle?

She spent the whole day after her speech nosing around — she came through O.P.D.[30] too & had her picture taken playing with dependent babies at Well Baby Clinic which happened to be going on today also with Col. Carlson in S[ick] O[fficers] Q[uarters].

I was hoping that some unconscious politico would invite her over to dine with us and unconsciously the menu planner would decide today would be the proper day this week for us to have cheese & coldcuts & orange punch — Oh well — give the Devil her due she undoubtedly means well. What griped me was that she'd let all those patients wait 3 hrs on her in the broiling sun. . . .

Love Like Always,

Bene

[30] Either the outpatient department or the outpatient dispensary.

"They are so glad to be going back to Civilization":
Victory and the Returning Vets

Both V-E Day (May 8, 1945) and V-J Day (August 15) resulted in great celebration around the world. Amid all the hoopla, servicemen and their loved ones had one big question: When would the servicemen be coming home?

Based on polls of more than 20,000 GIs, the army developed a point system for discharge: soldiers received one point for each month in the service, one point for each month spent overseas, five points for each campaign star or combat decoration (including the Purple Heart), and twelve points for each child. At eighty-five points, the soldier qualified for discharge.

Soldiers began to dream about what they would do after the war. Robert Isaksen said,"I never thought much about marriage till recently. It always seemed so far in the distance till I got in combat. Somehow that thought isn't so far off now because most of my thoughts for the future start when I get my discharge from the Army." Charles Gill wrote that he and his wife "are planning to enlarge our porch after the war and build a rootceller under it. I am having lots of fun planning the whole thing in my mind."

Soldiers returning from overseas spent a short time at an American base and then received their discharges. After the rigors of army discipline and the deprivations of combat service, camp life was relatively relaxed. While being processed in California, Warren Radke described this attitude: "Yesterday we were on a detail and I was given a hoe to slap down weeds but I didn't exactly kill myself. Tomorrow (Sunday) we're on K.P., everyone from master sergeants on down but as long as the boys are getting discharged no one's complaining."

Americans around the world shared many of the same emotions and experiences as the war ended, but the celebrations and reactions also differed. Tom Thomas, Charles Gill, Margaret Ebert, and Donald Gocker convey some of these varying perspectives.

Italy
May 7, 1945

Dear Mr. Broughton:

At last it's come. Tomorrow is VE day. And how does a soldier feel in a replacement depot training for the job of rifleman? Mighty happy, and mighty strange. The unconfirmed news came this afternoon as we were learning to launch rifle grenades against what was once a German Personnel Carrier. There was a little cheering, a lot of "let's wait and see if it's true", and then a lot more practice with the grenade launchers. You see we're all sweating out the Pacific, too. And then about half an hour ago shortly after supper the official announcement came. Everyone is smiles, and we'd all give our

Milwaukee Sentinel photo

Milwaukee residents take to the streets in celebration of V-J Day,
August 15, 1945.

beer ration to be in Rome tonight and see the celebration that must
be taking place.

In the latrine where most rumors begin, soldiers were trying to
figure up their adjusted service ratings, wondering if they had
enough points to get back to the blue serge suit hanging in the closet
back home. The T/3 beside me figured, "It must be about 2:30 in
the afternoon in Connecticut, and right now my wife is crying."
"Yeh," I answered, "and right now my mother is on the phone call-

ing my dad at the store and she's probably doing the same." And I was mighty proud. . . .

Stars and Stripes was the only Rome paper to carry the gruesome picture of Mussolini hanging by his heels like a carcass of beef. The Italian papers didn't have access to the plates, I guess. The entire edition was sold out in a matter of minutes. A quarter hour after it hit the streets Italian shoeshine boys were reselling the issue at black market prices up to 25 Lire each. Regular price is two Lire. . . .

Happy VE Day to you all and best wishes from your old friend

Tom Thomas

Charles H. Gill was born in Reedsburg (Sauk County) in 1912 and moved to Madison in 1929. He was employed at the Bank of Madison, where his father was the president, and was the father of two small children when he went on active duty with the navy in 1944. After training at Princeton and Harvard universities, he served as a lieutenant, junior grade, with the 7th Fleet in the South Pacific, stationed in New Guinea and the Philippines. He was discharged from active duty in March, 1946, and served in the reserves until 1954. He resumed his career in banking and later went into real estate before his death in 1961. While in the navy, he wrote often to his attorney and friend, Leon E. Isaksen.

Somewhere in the South Pacific
August 21, 1945

Dear Leon:

. . . I cannot agree that the surrender is a sufficient. As far as time is concerned the Japs were beaten regardless and it couldnt have lasted only a few more months. It would have cost a lot of American lives had we been forced to invade the home islands but I keep asking myself "Is it cheaper to lose a 1/4 million lives today or many millions in another 20 yrs." There is one way out and that is as you say The Allies must assume complete jurisdiction of Japan. If we fail in this we have failed in our intire war effort. I hope we are smart enough to take the power that is before us. . . .

Now that the war is over I feel that my duty is done. I am one of the older fellows who has no love for the military and will be less happy every month I am forced to remain in the service. If you want to see me home in the next y[ea]r you as my leagle adviser had better do some tall thinking and scratching of ones head to get me out. Now that the war is over I feel that I have fulfiled my obligation to the Country as far as the war is concerned. Marcy[31] defneatly needs me and Dad is not too happy about being forced to work as hard as

[31] Marcelle, his wife.

he does at his age. He feels that he doesnt want to hire anyone be-
cause I might return soon so the whole thing is a mess. . . .
Sincerely,
Charlie
C. H. Gill

Margaret Ebert was born in Rhinelander in 1917 and was living in Madison working at the *Wisconsin State Journal* when World War II started.
In September 1943, she joined the Red Cross as a recreation worker and
served in New Caledonia, Guadalcanal, and Hawaii. She left the Red
Cross in December, 1945, and became a junior high school teacher until
her marriage to Harry Kelk in 1955. They now operate a summer camp-
ground at Lake Tomahawk, in Oneida County.

Hawaii
September 6, 1945
Dear Mr. Anderson—
Greetings from the Hawaiian Islands! Time has slipped by and
brought me this much closer to Wisconsin and I hope to be there by
Christmas time. Red Cross has changed our time overseas from 24
months to 18 and by October 28 I will have completed 18 months in
the Pacific. I plan to give it up then. There will still be some Red
Cross work in these areas even though the War is over. As long as
there are troops out here there will be some kind of Red Cross service but I'm getting a bit homesick to see Mother and less interested
in this work. Guess I've caught the G.I. fever for "goin' home".
I came to Hawaii on June 1st from Guadalcanal. Since then I've
been working in a canteen on Hickam Field — night duty from
11:00 P.M. to 9:00 in the morning every *other* night. We serve cocoa-
Cola, pineapple juice, fresh sliced pineapple and coffee and doughnuts to airplane passengers of the Air Transport Command's big C-
54's. The loud speaker announces the departure of aircraft for
"Johnston, Kwajalein, Guam and Okinawa".[32] We've been waiting
to hear them add "Japan" after that last destination but it hasn't
happened yet. There is always a big gurgle of happiness from the
crowd when the departure is for "Hamilton Field, California."
Our customers come from all parts of the world but it is most fun
to wait on men from the fighting areas who have been out here 36 or
42 months and who "haven't seen a girl for two years". They are so
glad to be going back to Civilization. They come from all parts of
the Pacific. We call it "somewhere down under" but the G.I.'s say

---

[32] Allied-controlled Pacific islands, each closer to Japan than the last.

"that damn rock" which refers to any island they happened to be on.

In the morning P-38's take off on their practice runs and we can watch the B-29's come into John Rodgers Airport which adjoins Hickam Field. It is an interesting place to be but does not strike the same chord as being in a forward area or on one of those "damn rocks" where a canteen would seem like Broadway to the monotonous lives of service troops. I have been itching to go "down under" ever since the day I arrived. Or at least I was until the peace news came out. I had made arrangements with Red Cross and repacked my luggage to go to the Mariannas when the news broke and then I suddenly had a change of feeling and asked to stay until my time was up.

The first news of Japan's offer to accept the terms of the Potsdam agreement "*if*" came at 2:30 in the morning. All Hickam Field woke up and yelled. The ships in Pearl Harbor blew their sirens and horns

Three sailors join in the revelry in Milwaukee at the news that the war is over.

Milwaukee Journal photo

and screams came out of everywhere. A band marched up and down the streets playing "The Star Spangled Banner" and "You Are My Sunshine" with "California, Here I Come" for every other number. People followed it around in their pajamas. It was a completely spontaneous celebration and everything we've had since then has been a sort of anti-climax with nothing like the same feeling behind it. In fact our official V-J day celebration was almost drab everyone having completely worn themselves out and drained all their bottles beforehand.

I left New Caledonia for Guadalcanal in February and was there only three months. New Caledonia seemed haunted after the 25th Division left. By the way, Mr. Geo. Allingham, the R.C. Field Director I had worked with, was killed in the Luzon campaign. He was taking a coffee and doughnut run to the front lines when a mortar shell hit his jeep. I still get letters from men telling about the swell job he did — I believe he was awarded a bronze star. The whole division had a very rough time on Luzon. I'm still getting news of casualties among the groups I knew. The worst news came last December when the War Dept. listed my brother as "killed in action". For awhile I had a rather bad time over that. There is a good appreciation for the "cost of war" in all my thoughts these past few months.

Guadalcanal was horribly hot and not at all good for my Wisconsin constitution. It is hard to explain the effects of continued heat because we all worked and lived as though to ignore it. There were troops who had not left the island in 32 months. Some Red Cross girls had been there for 14 months. Some people were not bothered at all but there were others of us who felt like we were going mad and would soon be chewing off the tops of trees. I was certainly glad to leave but I did enjoy the time I spent there. I worked in a Rest Camp that provided programs and luxuries for men who had been on the island "too long".

Honolulu and Hickam Field seemed strange and hard to adjust to after 13 months "down under". In fact I think the adjustment back to normal life after living army style for a long time is even harder to make than getting used to the army. When service people started out they had the excitement and patriotic feelings of war to bolster them up and when they return they have feelings of resentment to hinder them. I have some understanding of the problems of returning service personnel. Of course, Hawaii isn't the United States as we know it but it is a very large step in that direction. The war has spoiled a lot of the "Romance of Hawaii" because it is so awfully crowded and busy and militarized. But I've been lucky enough to get a leave to the Island of Hawaii and have seen some less crowded spots where rural life and strange scenery had the real Hawaiian air. I saw Kilauea volcanoe and Halemaumau Crater. These aren't doing anything now but are still considered active and may erupt again in 1946. It was a very delightful trip but the one back to the mainland looks the best to me now.

Give my love to Florence and Sue.

Sincerely,
Margaret Ebert

Five months after the war in Europe ended, Roger Smith wrote his mother, Catherine Carney Smith, expressing his frustration and his eagerness to get home.

Biarritz
October 18, 1945

Dear Mom —

As usual the army is snafooed again on redeployment. Sure makes me disgusted to listen to their damned excuses. Marshal wants a big Army — he says so![33] I guess if the truth were known that's why we're still over here. It sure didn't take people long to decide wheather or not we could use boats to get over here on, But then I guess we can't blame Britain for not letting us use The Queens anymore if we won't even convert our own passenger boats to get troops home.[34] The guys sure boil under the collar when they read about fellows with 41 points getting out to play football, and who have never even left the states on that account also.

It's too much to swallow and the soldiers are sick of hearing excuses. Everyone at home worrying about "Getting the Veterines back on their feet."

Why in hell isn't someone a little more interested in "Getting us back" first! . . .

It's been pleasant here at Biarritz but the days drag any way. The other nite we saw a movie news reel. Pres Truman made a speech to

[33] General George C. Marshall, Army Chief of Staff. In testimony before the House Appropriations Committee made public on October 17, 1945, the general stated that the development of the atomic bomb had increased, rather than decreased, the need for a large military force.

[34] For the duration of the war, the British allowed the United States to use several large and fast ocean liners, the *Queen Elizabeth*, the *Queen Mary*, and the *Aquitania*, to transport soldiers and equipment to and from Europe. On Ocober 11, 1945, however, the British announced that the *Queen Elizabeth* and the *Aquitania* would be removed from American service and used to repatriate Canadians who had served in the war.

the men in service — soldiers here are as good a cross section of the Army as anywhere and they weren't at all pleased with the new President — in fact they booed and cast plenty of remarks.

Trumans delivery was very poor and when he said he knew all about what it was like over here and that he was a Captain in the Artillery in the last War, that was enough. He went on to say that he had seen the dead on the battle fields and the misery and all of that stuff — it didn't set well at all with anyone. The things the men wanted to know about he didn't have anything to say about.

I'm affraid if the men now in office are depending on a Veterines vote to put them in again they'll be very disappointed. They'll have to look to the Athletes and movie stars who they fixed discharges and soft set ups for — to vote them back in, it sure won't come from any of us I don't think.

Oh Well — they can't juggle us around for ever, if it keeps up for too long the boys will just up and find a way home for themselves or maybe ask out and settle down over here in Europe — You'd be surprised how easily they adapt themselves and learn the languages. Be sure though that if they stay, it won't be in the Army. On a pole in the E[uropean] T[heater of] O[perations] 61% of the officers said they'd stay in while only 3% of the E[nlisted] M[en] thought they'd consider it — Nuff Said! More soon, take it easy and don't over-work — go to bed early and get your sleep —

Love
Son Rog

Donald Gocker was born in 1927 in Beaver Dam and was a high school student when he enlisted in the navy in November, 1944. He became an electronic technician, second class, operating and maintaining radar, so-nar, and radar-detection devices on the *H. J. Ellison*, a destroyer, and the *William Powell*, a training ship. Gocker remained in the Navy until November, 1948, and then worked in advertising and printing in New York and Illinois until his retirement in 1988. He wrote to Joseph Helfert.

San Diego
October 10, 1945

Dear Joe,

This is the first chance I've had to write to you, and for the first time in my life, I am going to get serious and starting griping.

So this is the country that the world is supposed to look up to. So we are the fair haired boys that won the war, and showed that Democracy is the best form of government. Now the war is over, and everything has gone back to normal. When Amalgamated Fleas Incorporated goes out on strike, everything will be out. Joe, what chance am I going to have when I come back to civilian life? What chance is any 17 year old going to have? If he tries to get a job now employers will holler no education! When he gets out of College, this will be to the point where they will be saying once again "How much experience have you had?"

Right then and there Joe is when we are going to wish that we had never heard of political unions, and closed shops. Right there is when I and ten million other young fellows who want to live in the America that they fought for are going to raise hell like it's never been raised before.

Every day I pick up the paper and read where some other Corporation has had a walkout. Right below those headlines are the world series scores, and crowded in a corner on a back page we read the interesting news.

INTERNAL STRIFE HERE AND THERE!!!
WE WANT SO AND SO OUSTED*** THIS COUNTRY
WE WANT THIS AND THAT _ _ _ _ THAT COUNTRY

That's O.K. Joe, but doggone it, I'll bet the Detroit Tigers don't find a job for me when I get out of here, and those companies that made all that money during the war sure as heck aren't going to hire me for any worthwhile wage. The Union won't feed me when I'm hungry either, because they'll be too busy trying to get Mr Wartime Inflated Wages trying to strike for more money from the corporation that won't give it to them.

It appears to me that the only gain that we made out of the war was the fact that our cities weren't bombed. Our loss was that we can't try our war criminals. — Those boys who sit behind desks counting the money they made while us younger fellows tried to save their hides along with our own. When the bread line forms in a couple of years, let me know so that I can enlist again, and sail around the world trying to stay away from deplorable conditions.

I guess they don't figure that maybe five years from now I want to come home, get married and have a comfortable and pleasant life. They probably forget that my kids are the ones who will have to sweat out the next little piece of hell. I am lucky that I have got three years in here yet, think of the poor fellow who is coming back from the war to the thanks that he is getting from this supposedly free and great United States.

Things ain't the way they used to be, and they aren't the way they should have been. I thought of a little poem that has been bothering me ever since I left home, like a dope.

He who ventures from his doors,
In quest of forgotten foreign shores;
Will sometime without a doubt,
In some God-forsaken hole
Remember his venturing out
From home, his only true goal!

Yeah Joe, it's just a home and a little job that I want out of this mess, and I sure do hope that the people, through their power of voting will give it to me.

It sounds just like an editorial doesn't it Joe? Well, maybe that's what it's supposed to be.

I really do like the Navy, and Radar is a very interesting subject. Sometimes though, when a fellow looks back into the doorway of the life that he is fighting to get back into he wonders — I know I do

Sincerely,
Don

"The lessons to be learned from war are so simple"

After World War I, Americans had vowed that they would never be drawn into a global conflict again, trumpeting the virtues of "splendid isolationism" and putting faith in documents like the Kellogg-Briand pact, which was supposed to eliminate war forever. Yet less than twenty-five years later, millions of Americans fought World War II, which was longer and costlier (in terms of both money and lives) than the previous conflict. Throughout the war, many men and women in the service reflected on why it was necessary that they fight. Signe Skott Cooper recalled that "most Americans really thought that World War II was a worthy cause, that we had to get involved. . . . We felt it was right, it was right we should be doing this."

Americans, confident of their eventual triumph, possessed great optimism about the world of the future and about their ability to effect positive change in other areas of society. This sense of American accomplishment and confident outlook can be seen in letters reflecting on the war written by Peter G. Pappas (to Myrtle Trowbridge) and by Roy F. Bergengren, Jr. (to Don Anderson).

New Guinea
December 26, 1943
Dear Miss Trowbridge,
. . . The army is giving me an unrivalled education of travel; both coasts of the U.S.; Australia, New Guinea and a few more places in the future. All of us are learning how the other fellow lives — and we will know of life beyond our own group of states. I fervently hope our lesson is a lasting one for there is so much to be done after the war and we will need all of our wisdom and strength to meet the challenge to make this a decent world. At last we realize how fine a way of life we've had and how poor the rest of the world is — but with the material things must go spiritual forces which will breathe hope into the world.

I see I should have planned for a longer letter.

Eve Currie[35] writes in "Journey Among Warriors" that the other nations are fighting for the bright future while the American soldier, realizing how good his life has been, wants merely to return to his old way of life. Like any generalization it overlooks those painful exceptions; yet it contains much truth. On the whole our plane of living has been very high and it must be extended because a good life means much for a peaceful world. Still, we have much to take care of in our own backyard; poverty is not unknown; many are undernourished; there is much to be done in public health; education; housing and many other fields.

There are too many signs of intolerance and interest oppression — education still has much to accomplish. So, it appears that spiritual forces must walk hand in hand with material blessings.

There are favorable signs that the people of the U.S. are looking to activity in the sphere of world politics — a good omen but I wonder if it was not also true during the last war that there was much similar activity; many committees and numerous articles. Yet the results were lacking of any such ideas. I still believe the mass of voters exercise the greatest of powers and usually are quite intelligent. True, we blunder but the benefits of democracy far overweigh the shortcomings.

We have spent many hours talking of these problems and altho we agree on the objective to be reached, i.e. a world at peace and U.S. international participation we do not agree on the means — and that will be a pressing problem.

[35] Eve Curie, a French journalist, visited Allied forces fighting in Africa, the Middle East, Russia, and Asia between November, 1941, and April, 1942. She published her observations in *Journey Among Warriors* in 1943.

Yet our pressing and immediate problem is to win this war and then to meet the next problems. But we can not help but think of what is to come.

One hears much of any entanglement and red-tape but it goes its way and somehow manages to get things done — and I have found it takes good care of us. Under our present conditions I think we are well off — and altho our comforts are few we don't lack for the necessities — and life does become one of simple things. I never dreamt I could do things that I now accept as commonplace — and yet when I return I'll lose no time surrounding myself with the comforts of old.

War is a matter of much training; constant repetition of fundamentals and a lot of hot, dirty work. There is no glamour to it. . . .

Sincerely,

Peter

Italy

November 24, 1943

Dear Don,

. . . This will be my second Christmas overseas and I think I'm well qualified to report that the Yank, 1943 version, is doing a good job in upholding the traditions of his father and his grandfather and all who came before him. His few weaknesses are a source of pride rather than otherwise. He occasionally gets drunk, but that's because he loves his home and family and is terrifically lonely for both. He's slow to anger, but when he does get mad, he fights like hell. He's quick to forgive — the pictures of him giving his candy ration to Italian kids is not a publicity gag. Sometimes he gets cheated, but it's because he has a deep faith in human nature. I think he's the best there is.

We could have done very nicely without this war, but I do think it has given us a new sense of values which will go a long way in cancelling any future wars. We'll come out of it stronger than ever and with a revitalized conception of man's brotherhood to man which is, after all, what Christmas is all about. Next Christmas we overseas will demonstrate personally — at home.

Sincerely,

Roy

Germany
January 20, 1945
Dear Don,

Having entered Germany a while ago, I feel something like the coast-to-coast marathon runner must as he crosses the New York State line.

In 28 months, I've journeyed through 11 countries to get here. It was a rather roundabout route, but there's never been any doubt about where we were headed. I hope I shall travel right to Berlin — and then home.

So far, it has been an interesting, if unpleasant experience. I could certainly have done nicely without it; but since it has been necessary, I'm glad to be one of those taking a share in it.

There have been a few outstanding impressions. Obvious though they may be, they are none-the-less vivid.

First is the absolute futility of war. Seen at close range, it becomes so brutal and stupid that we have to rub our eyes to believe the world is capable of it. It can't be written; samples of the death, poverty, and destruction in war's wake must be seen to be appreciated.

In a Lyons café, a French journalist asked me,

"Why is it you Americans refuse to believe the Germans really tortured and killed so many innocent people in France?"

I couldn't answer. I guess it's because we live so far from such things and we must see to believe. Words fail to make such things real.

A second impression is the fundamental similarity of the peoples of the United Nations. I've lived and worked with British, French, Australian, South African, New Zealand, Polish, and Belgian soldiers to name a few. I'm convinced that we all seek the same general sort of life. We criticize one another for our little individual eccentricities; each of us thinks his is the best nation; but fundamentally we differ little. When this war is won, we must remember only the fundamentals and get together in a big way.

A third impression is that of America's own capabilities. London, Algiers, Paris, Rome, Florence, Marseilles, and every other city and town in every liberated country teeming with American traffic. Huge depots of American supplies, throngs of American men everywhere. If we can put forth one half the effort for peace that we've extended in this war, because it was necessary, there should never be need for another war. We must realize that peace, now, is just as necessary as the war has been.

I'm now living in a half-wrecked miner's house. There's snow and there's cold in addition to other little worrisome things. I and millions of others like me aren't enjoying ourselves at the moment, but we're perfectly willing to live this way because we have faith that the peoples of the world involved this time are going to do a better job in fashioning the peace. . . .

I've rambled on at some length and must now get a bit of shut-eye. The lessons to be learned from war are so simple and so obvious, that they have to come out. This time, dammit, we've got to remember them.

My best to the gang!
Roy

Suggestions for Further Reading and Location of Original Letters

The literature on the history of America's wars is voluminous; consequently, the following is intended as a highly selective list of suggestions for further reading on the topics in this volume.

Spanish-American War: David F. Trask, *The War With Spain in 1898* (New York, 1981) is a useful survey of the war. A contemporary account of the conflict in the Caribbean by a famous journalist is Richard Harding Davis, *The Cuban and Porto Rican Campaigns* (Freeport, N.Y., 1970; originally published in 1898). Don Russell, *Campaigning with King: Charles King, Chronicler of the Old Army*, edited and with an introduction by Paul L. Hedren (Lincoln, Neb., 1991) is a biography of a Wisconsin career soldier whose letters appear in this volume. The text, originally written in 1933, devotes only one chapter to King's service in the Philippine campaign, but is one of the few biographies of Wisconsin's Spanish-American War veterans that deals with the war.

World War I: Edward M. Coffman, *The War to End All Wars: The American Military Experience in World War I* (Madison, 1986) is a superb history of American involvement in the war that treats the social aspects of military life. It is complemented by David M. Kennedy, *Over Here: The First World War and American Society* (New York, 1980), which considers the impact of the war on American life. Lee Kennett, *The First Air War, 1914–1918* (New York, 1991) is concerned primarily with European aviation, but is important for understanding the air war because of the close attention it devotes to social and cultural developments. Many veterans published their recollections of the war. Two memoirs by veterans whose letters appear in this volume are William Mitchell, *Memoirs of World War I* (Westport, Conn., 1975; originally published as a series of magazine articles in 1928), and G. W. Garlock, *Tales of the Thirty-Second* (West Salem, Wis., 1927). Paul W. Glad, *The History of Wisconsin. Volume V: War, a New Era, and Depression, 1914–1940* (Madison, 1990) treats the war's impact in Wisconsin.

167

World War II: Lee Kennett, *G.I.: The American Soldier in World War II* (New York, 1987) is a well-written social history of the citizen-soldier that describes how military service affected the lives of millions of Americans who served during the Second World War. Geoffrey Perrett, *Days of Sadness, Years of Triumph: The American People, 1939–1945* (New York, 1973) provides an overview of life on the home front and examines both American unity and the cracks in the social façade during the war. D'Ann Campbell, *Women at War with America: Private Lives in a Patriotic Era* (Cambridge, Mass., 1984) discusses women in the work force, at home, and in the military. William F. Thompson, *The History of Wisconsin. Volume VI: Continuity and Change, 1940–1965* (Madison, 1988) offers an excellent account of Wisconsin during the war. The *Wisconsin Magazine of History* has published a number of articles on the war. One of the most moving of these is the record kept by a survivor of the Bataan death march: Ernest O. Norquist, "Three Years in Paradise: A GI's Prisoner-of-War Diary, 1942–1945," *WMH*, 63 (Autumn 1979), 3–35.

* * * * *

With the exception of the letters of Eldon J. Canright, Carl Jacobs, Charles King, and William Mitchell, all letters printed or quoted in this volume are from the manuscript collections of the State Historical Society of Wisconsin. The Canright letters are reprinted from the *Wisconsin Magazine of History*, 5 (1921–1922): 171–200, 301–319. The Jacobs, King, and Mitchell letters are in the Jacobs Papers at the Portage County Historical Society in Stevens Point, the King Papers at Carroll College in Waukesha, and the Mitchell Papers at the Library of Congress. Letters held by the State Historical Society may be found in collections bearing the writer's name, with the exception of the following:

World War I: Charles Brown Papers (Robert Whitney); William Hiestand Papers (Conrad Fox); and Albert J. O'Melia Papers (Walter A. Beaudette).

World War II: Don Anderson Papers (Duane Alexander, Roy F. Bergengren, Jr., Charles Birt, Margaret Ebert, Howard McCaffrey, Warren Radke, John D. "Pink" Rice, Carl Schluter, Harold J. Tidrow, F. L. "Woody" Weston); Mrs. Elmer Barr Papers (Russell Barr); Charles Broughton Papers (Tom Thomas); Minda Dockar Papers (Duane Molner, Louis F. Rodey); Lillian Otto Fried Papers (Roland Malcolm "Mac" Andresen, Thomas G. Boisclair, A. Roger Conant, Louis A. Schauer, David Schreiner); Joseph Helfert

Papers (Fred J. Draeger, Donald Gocker, Edward C. Hoyer, John Marthaler, Leo Pietrucha, John F. Polchinski, William L. Schlicher); Leon E. Isaksen Papers (Vivian Croake, Charles H. Gill, Robert Isaksen); Horace Smith Family Papers (Margaret J. "Bene" Smith, Mark W. Smith, Roger G. Smith); and Myrtle Trowbridge Papers (Paul Hassett, Le Roy "Whitey" Holm, John Koetting, Ole Oines, Peter Pappas).

Quotations from Signe Skott Cooper, Loa Fergot, and Luida E. Sanders are from interviews in the Wisconsin Women during World War II Oral History Project, which are deposited at the State Historical Society. Photographs identified with WHi negative numbers are from the State Historical Society's collections.

Index

170